MIDI Sequencing in Reason™:
Skill Pack

Steve Nalepa

THOMSON

COURSE TECHNOLOGY™

Professional ■ Technical ■ Reference

MIDI Sequencing
in Reason™:
Skill Pack

Publisher and General Manager, Thomson Course Technology PTR: Stacy L. Hiquet

Associate Director of Marketing: Sarah O'Donnell

Manager of Editorial Services: Heather Talbot

Marketing Manager: Mark Hughes

Senior Editor: Mark Garvey

Development Editor: Orren Merton

Project Editor: Kate Shoup Welsh

Technical Reviewer: Vince Fierro

PTR Editorial Services Coordinator: Erin Johnson

Copy Editor: Kate Shoup Welsh

Interior Layout: Shawn Morningstar

Cover Designer: Mike Tanamachi

CD-ROM Producer: Brandon Penticuff

Indexer: Katherine Stimson

Proofreader: Steve Honeywell

Reason is a trademark of Propellerhead Software. All other trademarks are the property of their respective owners.

Important: Thomson Course Technology PTR cannot provide software support. Please contact the appropriate software manufacturer's technical support line or Web site for assistance.

Thomson Course Technology PTR and the author have attempted throughout this book to distinguish proprietary trademarks from descriptive terms by following the capitalization style used by the manufacturer.

Information contained in this book has been obtained by Thomson Course Technology PTR from sources believed to be reliable. However, because of the possibility of human or mechanical error by our sources, Thomson Course Technology PTR, or others, the Publisher does not guarantee the accuracy, adequacy, or completeness of any information and is not responsible for any errors or omissions or the results obtained from use of such information. Readers should be particularly aware of the fact that the Internet is an ever-changing entity. Some facts may have changed since this book went to press.

Educational facilities, companies, and organizations interested in multiple copies or licensing of this book should contact the Publisher for quantity discount information. Training manuals, CD-ROMs, and portions of this book are also available individually or can be tailored for specific needs.

ISBN-10: 1-59863-182-9

ISBN-13: 978-1-59863-182-1

Library of Congress Catalog Card Number: 2006920356

Printed in the United States of America

07 08 09 10 11 TW 10 9 8 7 6 5 4 3 2

THOMSON

COURSE TECHNOLOGY

Professional ■ Technical ■ Reference

Thomson Course Technology PTR, a division of Thomson Learning Inc. 25 Thomson Place Boston, MA 02210

http://www.courseptr.com

This book is dedicated:

To Mom and Dad, for their love and support

To Calvin Banks, for his inspiration and wisdom

To Mark Garvey, for his encouragement and friendship

# Acknowledgments

Writing this book has been a great adventure, and I would like to thank a number of wonderful people who have been an incredible inspiration to me along the way, as well as the amazing crew of editors who helped make this book possible.

First, I would like to thank my parents for always being there for me. My grandmother bought me a Lowrey organ from the corner organ store in the mall when I was five years old, and in order to get the bigger, better organ in first grade, I had to agree to take eight years of organ lessons. Well, it was great for a while, but as I got older and my little buddies were outside playing sports, the last thing I wanted to be doing was finger exercises to a metronome. However, the reality is that this visionary move was one of the best things that could have happened to me, for it laid down the musical foundation for everything I would do afterward. From day one, no matter what path I've chosen to pursue, whether it was starting an art-book publishing company or working as a paranormal news researcher, my mom and dad have always been there for me, and I feel supremely blessed to have such beautiful, loving parents.

Next, I'd like to thank the amazing Lili Haydn. Her profound musical talent has been an incredible inspiration for me; she is arguably the most extraordinary violinist on the planet today—"Jimmy Hendrix on the violin," as George Clinton calls her. Her live performances are beyond words. Collaborating with her musically opened up so many doors for me as an artist, and I will be forever grateful for all the lessons that I learned from her. If it weren't for Lili recommending me to Calvin Banks for a tech-support position at M-Audio, I probably would not be here today putting the finishing touches on this book.

Calvin Banks is a profound and extremely deep human being, a beacon of light, love, and wisdom in this world. He has been an incredible friend and mentor for me. He has had an immensely positive influence in my life, and I have learned so much from him. His strength and courage have encouraged me to be a better person, and his example gives me great hope for the future. Thank you, Calvin. Thanks also to all my friends at M-Audio tech support; I will always cherish the good times we had saving the world one call at a time.

There are a number of people who helped me get through this production; without their help, this project would not be possible. I'd first like to thank Mark Garvey for all of his encouragement, and especially for providing me with some wonderful opportunities. Mark has been a great friend. I am really glad I decided to go DJ for free up at the Xtreme Game Developers Xpo in Silicon Valley, where we first met, a few years back! This was one of those notable moments in life where things take a very positive turn and you can trace it back and pinpoint the exact moment. Thanks, Mark.

Orren Merton is an incredible editor, and his guidance and input helped kick-start this project out of neutral. His outline-development skills are supreme, and he really helped me actualize this project. Kate Welsh is a fantastic project editor, and she took the ball and ran with it. She did a hell of a job cleaning everything up and making it flow. Kate, you rock! Likewise, Vince Fierro did a fantastic job as the technical editor on this project, and I am happy to see that he has been carrying the comedic torch in M-Audio tech support since I moved on to marketing. Working the phones in a tech-support department is a little bit like getting paid to take comedy improv lessons. Humor diffuses the stress, and Vince is a rising star. Thank you so much for all your help. Oh, and nice shoes. Thank you to Raul Resendiz, Evan 'Bluetech', Casey Kim and Duncan Laurie for granting us permission to include some demo content from their loop libraries.

I would like to thank all of my friends who were supportive during the production of the book. In particular, I'd like to thank Sariah Storm for all of her inspiration. We've been producing multi-media events together for a few years now, and I have learned so much thanks to her. There's a deep and inspired connection there, and I am completely grateful that she is my friend. To my good friends and old roommates RD and Phil: Thanks for putting up with me during my stressful first attempt at this project. I also want to thank John Von Seggern, Susan Mainzer, Michael Backes, Shana Nys Dambrot, Coco Conn, AJ, and all of the amazing people who make living in Los Angeles such a beautiful experience. Also, big ups to Sascha Lewis, David Last, David Lublin, Benton-C Bainbridge, Aerostatic, and the rest of my New York crew for keeping me continually inspired.

To everyone at M-Audio, thank you so much for making the day job so much fun. I couldn't ask for a better gig, although it would be nice if the office were closer to town! As far as the quality of the people who work there, M-Audio is an extraordinary place to work. Big thanks to everyone who makes the experience there so joyful, especially my chuck wagon buddies Greg Williams, Peter Schmidt, and Elliott Chenault. Also, thanks to Adam Castillo, Kevin Walt, and Woody Moran for their encouragement and guidance. Thanks to KD for the big smiles and good vibes; Chad Carrier for his brilliant creations; shAmii wAttz:on for always making things interesting; Ryan and Roland for being a source of knowledge on demand; and Jeff, Sal, Aaron, Raul, Kashan and everyone who has been there in the trenches with me. Special thanks to Duane Morris for spreading the use of the word "bushwhack" and starting a linguistic revolution, and for turning me on to Sambazon Organic Acai drinks.

Finally, I would like to sincerely thank Matt Piper. He's been right there with me in the trenches, writing his own book in parallel, and I don't know if I would have made it through this project with my sanity if it wasn't for Matt and our friendship, laughter, and musical outpourings. Matt, going to see Radiohead at Bonnaroo was a fantastic idea. That was truly epic.

About the Author

Electronic musician, multimedia event producer, art-book publisher, and mad-scientist collector, **Steve Nalepa** has explored a range of territories, but his first love has always been music. Based in Los Angeles, Nalepa is a producer, programmer, keyboardist, and sound designer who has collaborated with world-renowned artists from across the musical spectrum, including producer Bill Laswell, saxophonist Pharoah Sanders, violinist Lili Haydn, and funk legend George Clinton, among others.

After graduating from Yale in 1994 with a degree in Economics and Mathematics and a spot on the Academic All-Ivy Football Team, Nalepa moved to Los Angeles where he taught high-school math and science, worked in TV and film production, and held a position as paranormal news researcher for the national daily show *Strange Universe*. Nalepa and two friends then founded the art-book publishing company Dilettante Press, ultimately publishing award-winning books and producing exhibitions and multimedia events at museums and art galleries around the world.

Currently the Technical Marketing Specialist for M-Audio, Nalepa is the resident Ableton Live expert, teaches clinics on Live and Pro Tools M-Powered, and provides VIP technical support for sponsored artists and journalists. He was also the Technical Support Supervisor and lead Reason expert while M-Audio distributed the Propellerhead software. He is an experienced teacher, technical writer, and instructional-video producer who recently wrote and produced *Reason 3 CSi Master* and contributed to *Ableton Live 4 CSi Master*.

Nalepa recently completed his debut album *Flatlands* and was featured on the compilations *Left Coast Liquid* and *Beneath the Surface* from Native State Records and *Future Sound Theory* from Celestial Dragon. On the horizon, Nalepa is working on his second album while compiling a *Flatlands* DVD featuring visual interpretations from a formidable roster of ten video artists. He begins teaching a Principles of Music Technology class in the fall at Chapman University School of Music.

Table of Contents

Contents

X

Introduction

Welcome to MIDI Sequencing in Reason

Gone are the days when big budgets and access to a massive recording studio were required to get into the recording game. These days, thanks to advances in computer technology and to the development of recording software like Reason, more and more professional music is being created at home. All it takes is a computer, a good sound card, a set of quality studio monitors or headphones, a MIDI controller, strong musical ideas, and, of course, Reason, you are ready to go.

Reason comes complete with numerous fantastic synthesizers, samplers, drum machines, mixers, and effects that can be wired together in an infinite number of ways. Using Reason is like having an expandable dream studio, without a massive mess of cables cluttering up your space. It's a complete virtual studio, a powerful MIDI application with endless creative possibilities...assuming you know how to use it. Indeed, the key to producing and composing in Reason is learning how to master the tools available to you in the MIDI sequencer. This book is your guide to unlocking the power and creative freedom available in this dynamic program.

How This Book Works

This book will teach you how to use all the major features of Reason's sequencer. All of the available tools and functions will be introduced and explained, with step-by-step explanations of the various ways to use them to enhance your productions. A key part of this *Skill Pack* is the CD-ROM included with this book. It's full of sample content and examples that you will use to build a song from scratch and, in the process, learn all the MIDI-sequencing intricacies of this dynamic and flexible software.

Who This Book Is For

MIDI Sequencing in Reason: Skill Pack is for anyone anxious to master production skills in Reason. If you are a hip-hop producer, a film or TV composer, a singer/songwriter, an electronic music producer, or a remix artist—whether you are just getting started or you are a pro looking to master your skills—this book is for you.

What You'll Learn

This book will help you master Reason's sequencer. After reading this book, you will have a thorough understanding of all the features this application offers to help you compose and edit your music. Here are just a few topics you'll explore:

- You'll start with a brief history of MIDI, tracing the development of the sequencer—from separate hardware to integrated software.

- You'll get an overview of the Reason sequencer and its two main modes: Arrange and Edit.

- You'll be introduced to the editing tools available to you in the sequencer and will learn about the different lanes of data displayed in the sequencer.

- You'll then look at the various ways to get note data into the Reason sequencer: by drawing them in using the Pencil tool or playing them in with a MIDI controller.

- You'll take an in-depth look at the Snap to Grid feature and learn how to best use it when drawing in notes, no matter which device you are working with.

- You'll explore Reason's Quantize Notes During Recording feature, which, when turned on, automatically constrains incoming MIDI notes to a grid that you define.

- You'll explore your options for sequencing beats in Reason using the Redrum Drum Computer (a 10-channel drum computer with 32 step-programmable patterns) and the Dr REX Loop Player (which provides a quick way to build a structural framework for your song).

- You'll explore the various tools available to edit your MIDI data once you have entered it into the sequencer. You'll learn how to correct mistakes, move and duplicate notes and events, and delete events using the Eraser tool, as well as use the Change Events dialog box to take a selected group of MIDI data and then transpose it, scale the velocity of the notes, add or subtract a specific amount of velocity, scale the tempo, and more.

- You'll learn about recording parameter automation and will examine the tools available to edit velocity and controller data in the MIDI sequencer.

- You'll discover how to create linear velocity ramp-ups, controller curves, and non-linear curves.

- You'll examine Reason's Quantization function, which allows you to tighten up a recorded drumbeat, correct mistakes, or alter a programmed beat to give it a different feel.

- You'll work with Reason's Capture User Groove function, which enables you to extract the feel of one part of your song and apply it to another.

- You'll wrap everything up with a discussion about mixing your finished song, and use Reason's fantastic mastering plug-ins to create professional quality music.

When all is said and done, you'll be well on your way to recording your grooves the easy way—with Reason.

MIDI and the Modern Sequencer

This chapter provides an introduction to MIDI and traces the development of the sequencer. One of the important outcomes of the creation and widespread adoption of the MIDI protocol has been the development of hardware and computer-based sequencers, which can be used to record, edit, and play back musical performances. These sequencers have evolved from analog hardware units, to humble software programs on the fastest computers of their day (meager by today's standards), to the massively powerful versions you see on the market today.

Introduction to MIDI

The development of the MIDI specification in the early 1980s enabled synthesizers, samplers, sound cards, drum machines, and computers from all different manufacturers to effectively communicate with one another, sync together, and exchange system information. In the 1970s, before MIDI, it was not uncommon to see a massive wall of hardware synthesizers at a rock concert. After the advent of MIDI, the development of rack-mountable versions of many synthesizers allowed a performer to use only one controller keyboard as his main performance center, sending the data out of it to trigger all the other sound modules. The development of MIDI coincided with the development of personal computers, which led to the development of software sequencers. Reason takes this concept even one step further, combining the sequencer with software synthesis, putting a powerful virtual synthesizer and sampler rack right inside your computer.

What Is MIDI?

MIDI stands for *Musical Instrument Digital Interface*. Wikipedia defines it this way: "MIDI is an industry-standard electronic communications protocol that defines each musical note in an electronic musical instrument such as a synthesizer, precisely and concisely, allowing electronic musical instruments and computers to exchange data, or 'talk,' with each other. MIDI does not transmit audio—it simply transmits digital information about a musical performance."

I

MIDI is the brainchild of Dave Smith, audio engineer and founder of legendary synthesizer company Sequential Circuits. He presented a paper to the Audio Engineering Society in 1981 promoting a Universal Synthesizer Interface (USI), based on discussions in his meetings with Tom Oberheim and Ikutaro Kakehashi of Roland. Companies around the world worked together to refine USI into a more powerful standard, and MIDI Specification 1.0 was published in August 1983. MIDI quickly became the industry standard, revolutionizing the way music was made and how musical instruments communicated with each other.

Sequential Circuits was instrumental in the development of MIDI. In late 1982, Sequential released the world's first MIDI synthesizer: the Prophet 600. At the 1983 annual NAMM music tradeshow, Dave Smith gave the very first public demonstration of this new MIDI protocol, showing the Prophet 600 successfully communicating with the Roland JX-3P (see Figure 1.1).

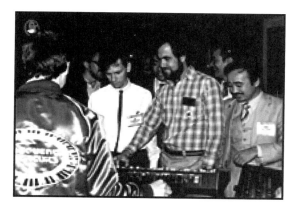

Figure 1.1
Dave Smith debuting MIDI at NAMM, 1983.

How MIDI Works

When a musician plays a note on a MIDI keyboard, the instrument transmits a MIDI message serially out of the MIDI OUT Port. The data travels through a MIDI cable, and into the MIDI IN port on another synthesizer or sound module (see Figure 1.2). It can also be routed into the MIDI IN port on a MIDI interface connected to a computer. These days, there is a plethora of MIDI controllers that transmit this MIDI data through a USB or FireWire cable into the computer, communicating with an audio application via a software driver. A number of manufacturers, such as M-Audio, Evolution, E-MU, Edirol, Korg, Alesis, and Novation, are making USB MIDI keyboards of all shapes and sizes, all of which can be used with Reason.

A transmitted MIDI message contains information stored in one or more single-byte binary numbers. Although the bandwidth of MIDI cable is limited, there is more than enough to transmit the compact MIDI messages. These messages are small for another reason as well: to keep the *latency* down to a minimum. When working with MIDI, even a very slight delay from the time you trigger the keyboard until the time you hear the sound can throw off your timing. This delay is known as *latency*.

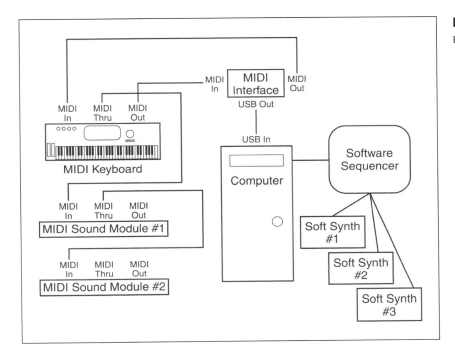

Figure 1.2
How MIDI works.

MIDI Cables

MIDI data is generally transmitted over a MIDI cable. The standard MIDI cable comes in various lengths and colors, with male plugs with a five-pin DIN connection featured on each end (see Figure 1.3). The standard MIDI specification suggests that the maximum length of a MIDI cable is 50 feet, although people have been known to build their own custom cables and achieve longer distances. A quick Internet search reveals a number of web sites with directions on how to achieve this.

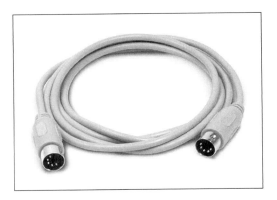

Figure 1.3
A standard MIDI cable.

3

What is Latency?

Latency can be defined as the lag time between the instant a note is struck and instant the sound associated with that note is heard. It is a fairly common issue when working with computer-based audio systems. It is important to optimize your machine and adjust the settings in your sound card's control panel before beginning a project. Often, the built-in sound card will not have an adjustable buffer size, leaving you unable to lower the overall latency. Professional sound cards, however, give you the ability to lower the buffer size and thus decrease the lag time between striking a note and hearing the sound that comes out of your computer.

If you set the buffer size too small and you have a big project open with a lot of CPU-intensive instruments and effects, your computer may not be able to properly process all the audio, resulting in pops and clicks, dropout, or distortion. Increasing a sound card's buffer size essentially gives your computer more time to process the sound before spitting it out of the computer, but it comes with increased latency. There are a number of useful optimization tips on the following web sites to help you realize the best performance with your PC:

- http://www.musicxp.net/tuning_tips.php
- http://www.pcaudiolabs.com/setuptips.asp

In addition, the following web site features a number of good suggestions for optimizing OSX for audio production:

- http://www.jakeludington.com/ask_jake/
  20050523_optimize_mac_os_x_for_audio_recording.html

Velocity

Velocity is a type of MIDI message that technically measures how fast a player presses a key on the keyboard. It is somewhat similar to volume in that lesser values result in quieter sounds. Velocity essentially measures how hard the player hits the keys, and its value ranges from 0–127. Keys played softly are pressed down more slowly and will have lower values, resulting in softer sounds. Striking a key more quickly results in a higher velocity and a generally louder sound, while a key struck at full force will yield a velocity of 127.

Some MIDI keyboards feature a choice of different velocity curves. A *velocity curve* is a parameter that determines how sensitive the keys will be to the incoming velocity values, thus altering the feel or responsiveness of the keyboard. A fixed velocity curve will generate the same velocity value no matter how hard you strike a key.

Note On/Note Off Messages

When a key is struck on a MIDI keyboard, a 'Note On' message is sent corresponding to the timing of the key being struck that says that this specific note was played at this specific time. When a key is released, a 'Note Off' message is sent at the exact time it is released.

If a keyboard has an aftertouch feature, another parameter is transmitted between the Note On and Note Off messages that states whether the user has changed the force with which he is holding down the key. This aftertouch parameter is then assigned to alter the sound in some way, perhaps altering a filter.

MIDI Channels

The standard MIDI protocol allows you to transmit up to 16 channels of data. A *MIDI channel* is a discrete portion of the complete MIDI signal. Each of the 16 individual channels carries an independent message. A MIDI instrument can be configured to receive data on any one of these 16 channels, similar to the way that a television can be tuned in to one of the various channels. Thus, one MIDI cable can carry MIDI data on the different channels to trigger different melodies for different sounds.

Instruments that can receive multiple channels at once and respond to them are called *multi-timbral*. This type of instrument can receive 16 channels of MIDI data over one MIDI cable, each channel set to trigger a different patch simultaneously. There are a number of multi-timbral synthesizers on the market, as well as software synthesizers often referred to as *soft synths*. Reason's MIDI IN device at the very top of the rack gives you the ability to receive and route 16 channels of MIDI information to trigger 16 different devices.

MIDI IN, MIDI OUT, MIDI THRU

Most instruments that support MIDI include both MIDI IN and MIDI OUT ports, and many also feature a MIDI THRU port. If you are playing a hardware synth that supports MIDI and would like to simultaneously trigger the sounds on another synth or sound module that also supports MIDI, you would route a MIDI cable from the MIDI OUT of the synth you are actually playing to the MIDI IN on the other synth or sound module. When you play a note on the one keyboard, it will simultaneously trigger the same note on the other device.

If you wanted to chain together several MIDI synthesizers, you would utilize the MIDI THRU port. You would first route a cable from the MIDI OUT on the synth you are actually playing to the MIDI IN on the second synth. You would then route a MIDI cable out the MIDI THRU port on this second synth to the MIDI IN port on a third synth (see Figure 1.4). In this way, the MIDI data is literally passed through the second synth to the third synth. The MIDI THRU port simply echoes the signal coming into the MIDI IN port. Thus, when you trigger a note on the first keyboard, it will actually play the same corresponding note on both the second and third keyboards.

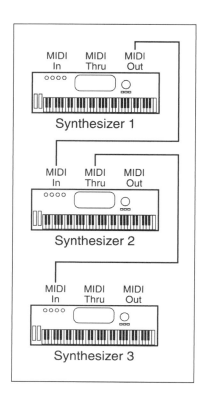

Figure 1.4
Chaining several synths together with MIDI.

General MIDI

In September of 1991, the MIDI Manufacturers Association and the Japan MIDI Standards Committee launched a new era in MIDI technology when they adopted a universal specification called General MIDI (GM). General MIDI is a set of requirements for MIDI devices geared toward ensuring consistent playback performance on all devices that bear the GM logo. Some of these requirements include at least 24-voice polyphony, support for all 16 MIDI channels, key-based percussion always on MIDI channel 10, and some various defined continuous controller mapping assignments. For example, a MIDI controller that has a CC (continuous controller) value of 7 will always control the volume on a GM sound module. There must also be a minimum of 128 preset instruments conforming to the GM Instrument Patch Map (see Table 1.1). Basically, all music written and sequenced in General MIDI should play back with the same instrument sound on any General MIDI sound source.

Table 1.1   General MIDI Instrument Patch Map

Piano

1 Acoustic Grand Piano

2 Bright Acoustic Piano

3 Electric Grand Piano

4 Honky Tonk Piano

5 Electric Piano 1

6 Electric Piano 2

7 Harpsichord

8 Clavinet

Organ

17 Drawbar Organ

18 Percussive Organ

19 Rock Organ

20 Church Organ

21 Reed Organ

22 Accordion

23 Harmonica

24 Tango Accordion

Bass

33 Acoustic Bass

34 Electric Bass (Finger)

35 Electric Bass (Pick)

36 Fretless Bass

37 Slap Bass 1

38 Slap Bass 2

39 Synth Bass 1

40 Synth Bass 2

Chromatic Percussion

9 Celesta

10 Glockenspiel

11 Music Box

12 Vibraphone

13 Marimba

14 Xylophone

15 Tubular Bells

16 Dulcimer

Guitar

25 Nylon String Guitar

26 Steel String Guitar

27 Electric Jazz Guitar

28 Electric Clean Guitar

29 Electric Muted Guitar

30 Overdriven Guitar

31 Distortion Guitar

32 Guitar Harmonics

Solo Strings

41 Violin

42 Viola

43 Cello

44 Contrabass

45 Tremolo Strings

46 Pizzicato Strings

47 Orchestral Strings

48 Timpani

7

Table 1.1   General MIDI Instrument Patch Map *(continued)*

Ensemble	Brass
49 String Ensemble 1	57 Trumpet
50 String Ensemble 2	58 Trombone
51 SynthStrings 1	59 Tuba
52 SynthStrings 2	60 Muted Trumpet
53 Choir Aahs	61 French Horn
54 Voice Oohs	62 Brass Section
55 Synth Voice	63 SynthBrass 1
56 Orchestra Hit	64 SynthBrass 2

Reed	Pipe
65 Soprano Sax	73 Piccolo
66 Alto Sax	74 Flute
67 Tenor Sax	75 Recorder
68 Baritone Sax	76 Pan Flute
69 Oboe	77 Blown Bottle
70 English Horn	78 Skakuhachi
71 Bassoon	79 Whistle
72 Clarinet	80 Ocarina

Synth Lead	Synth Pad
81 Lead 1 (Square)	89 Pad 1 (New Age)
82 Lead 2 (Sawtooth)	90 Pad 2 (Warm)
83 Lead 3 (Calliope)	91 Pad 3 (Polysynth)
84 Lead 4 (Chiff)	92 Pad 4 (Choir)
85 Lead 5 (Charang)	93 Pad 5 (Bowed)
86 Lead 6 (Voice)	94 Pad 6 (Metallic)
87 Lead 7 (Fifths)	95 Pad 7 (Halo)
88 Lead 8 (Bass + Lead)	96 Pad 8 (Sweep)

Table 1.1 General MIDI Instrument Patch Map *(continued)*

Synth Effects	Ethnic
97 FX1 (Rain)	105 Sitar
98 FX 2 (Soundtrack)	106 Banjo
99 FX 3 (Crystal)	107 Shamisen
100 FX 4 (Atmosphere)	108 Koto
101 FX 5 (Brightness)	109 Kalimba
102 FX 6 (Goblins)	110 Bagpipe
103 FX 7 (Echoes)	111 Fiddle
104 FX 8 (Sci-Fi)	112 Shanai
Percussive	**Sound Effects**
113 Tinkle Bell	121 Guitar Fret Noise
114 Agogo	122 Breath Noise
115 Steel Drums	123 Seashore
116 Woodblock	124 Bird Tweet
117 Taiko Drum	125 Telephone Ring
118 Melodic Tom	126 Helicopter
119 Synth Drum	127 Applause
120 Reverse Cymbal	128 Gunshot

MIDI Is Not Audio

When you are recording MIDI, you are not actually recording audio. Rather, you are recording information about when a note was struck, how hard it was struck (velocity), and when it was released. Unlike audio, this recorded note information can then be edited and fine-tuned, as well as reassigned to a different instrument or sound source. Don't like the bass sound? No problem, just reassign the recorded MIDI performance to trigger a different sound. With audio recording, you would need to go through and re-record the entire performance. Working with MIDI, you can keep a great performance even though you change your mind about the sound selection.

History of Sequencing

A crucial development in the early 70s was the creation of larger and larger sequencers. These earliest sequencers consisted of arrays of knobs that would be activated one at a time, each one set to output a specific voltage, producing a cyclical pattern of voltages. These voltage-controlled analog sequencers paved the way for what was to come. The underlying circuitry that made up these sequences was essentially digital, and designers began to look into ways of taking advantage of the exciting new technology.

Sequencing began with analog hardware devices utilizing the concept of voltage control. Through the development of microprocessors, sequencing evolved with the development of the Roland TB-303, TR-808, and TR-909. These pattern-programmable devices had rock-solid timing and utilized a step sequencer. The TB-303 BassLine, known for its signature acid squeal, became a favorite of dance producers. The 808 preceded the 909, and was a major breakthrough for pattern sequencing, yet its electronic sounds were initially frowned upon, and the device quickly ended up in bargain bins. Adopted by cash-strapped techno producers, the 808 enjoyed an incredible second coming and is now one of the most sought-after pieces of hardware.

The sequencing revolution continued with significant developments by Akai and E-MU, especially the popular Akai MPC-60 MIDI Production Center and its successors. The evolution continued with the development of digital audio workstations such as the Roland VS series, eventually leading to fully integrated workstations such as the Korg Triton. Meanwhile, personal computers appeared back in the early 80s, coinciding with the development of MIDI, which led to the creation of software-based sequencers.

Voltage Control

In the 1960s and 1970s, before the invention of the MIDI specification, the sequencer was actually a hardware unit that would connect to a synthesizer and automatically play a repeating sequence of notes. Synthesizers were still analog devices at this time, most of them relying on the concept of voltage control, invented by the legendary Robert Moog. The pitch of a note played on a voltage-controlled analog synthesizer is directly proportional to the amount of applied input voltage, thus giving each note a recordable value in volts. Many of these synthesizers conformed to a standard amount of 1 volt/octave. A hardware sequencer could connect up with a synthesizer and provide the appropriate output voltage level, which could then be changed at each step as it progressed to the next note in the sequence.

Some synthesizers even went as far as to include their own built-in sequencer. Early versions were of the modular variety. A nice example of this is the Roland Corporation's massive System 700 Modular Synthesizer. The synthesizer's 717A module, Roland's very first sequencer, was one of the most complex voltage-controlled analog sequencers ever made.

These early sequencers were a major breakthrough for electronic musicians of the time, but they were also somewhat limited. There were limitations in the length of the sequence as well as the restricting nature of using repeating sequences. Attempting to use a note value of anything other than completely regular values also caused timing problems. Still, restrictions aside, these devices were utilized with fantastic results by artists such as Tangerine Dream, Jean-Michel Jarre, Klaus Schulze, and Kraftwerk.

The Roland TB-303, TR-808, and TR-909

Roland Corporation continued to push the boundaries by creating a number of pattern-programmable devices, developing several units that have grown to become legends even though they were initially not very popular. Roland's TR-808 and TR-909 drum machines and the TB-303 BassLine were fully programmable, allowing you to create sequences on them. Their subsequent adoption by dance and hip-hop producers turned these devices into highly sought-after units.

The TB-303 features a very simple step-time method for entering note data into the 16-step programmable sequencer. It was, however, notoriously challenging to use, and often would result in different outcomes than intended. Some users took advantage of the unit's quirkiness, especially the way its programmed patterns would randomly vary if the batteries were removed for a stretch of time, which became part of the device's signature sound.

The TR-808, the first fully programmable drum machine, was an important step in the evolution of sequencers. Originally disregarded because of its artificial, synthetic drum sounds, the birth and runaway success of techno combined with its producers' widespread use of the device completely turned things around; the 808, which had rock-solid timing, became one of the most popular drum machines of all time.

Roland's TR-909 retained the TR808's programming method, which involved selecting a sound and then placing the beats utilizing the 16 buttons across the bottom of the unit. Just as with the 808, the 909 was not met with the initial enthusiasm Roland hoped for, and, like the 808, it too ended up becoming a highly sought-after unit.

The Akai MPC-60

In 1982, Roger Linn's LinnDrum was the device that brought about the early end of the TR-808's run. After the demise of Linn Electronics, Roger Linn collaborated with Akai in the design of a top-of-the-line sampling drum machine. Linn's newer creation, the MPC-60 (see Figure 1.5), featured a 64-channel sequencer, powerful quantization options, a large display, and many different sync options.

Figure 1.5
The Akai MPC-60.

The Akai MPC-60 is one of the most famous drum machines and sequencers in the world. It quickly became a must-have for all hip-hop, R&B, industrial, and electronic music. Coveted for its feel and unique swing, many famous beats have been produced with the MPC-60. It has an almost cult-like following among hip-hop producers.

The Roland VS Series

The evolution continued on the hardware side with the development of the Roland VS series. The Roland VS hard-disk recorder is a hardware unit that allows users to record, edit, process, and mix multiple tracks of audio. These devices allow you to sequence both audio and MIDI, and have evolved with each subsequent release, growing from the original VS-880 into the powerful VS-2480 of today.

The VS-880 sounded better than many other recorders available at the time, and it was loaded with features. It became incredibly popular, taking sequencing to a whole new level. The speed of computers grew as did storage capacity, and software sequencers eventually won out because of their ease of navigation.

Digital Workstations

It is also important to mention the development of complete digital workstations. The Korg M1 was the first widely known workstation, and it was a huge seller for Korg—the best-selling digital keyboard of all time, in fact, outselling the Yamaha DX7 and Roland D-50. The M1 featured an on-board MIDI sequencer and a wide palette of sounds that allowed musicians to produce complete, professional arrangements. The very first workstation was the Ensoniq ESQ-1.

The Korg Triton (Figure 1.6) continued this tradition. It is another popular keyboard workstation that features a built-in sequencer, diverse onboard sounds, and a powerful sampler. The Triton's built-in 16-track sequencer features an over-200,000 note capacity, and it quickly became an incredibly popular unit for both live performance and studio work.

Figure 1.6
The Korg Triton.

Software MIDI Sequencers

The origin of today's popular MIDI sequencers goes back to the initial wave of home computers in the early 1980s—the days of the Commodore 64, early Macintosh systems, and the Atari ST computer. These were the first machines that were fast enough to actually run these programs. You have to remember: Machines back then were nowhere near today's blazing fast home computers, nor did they have anywhere near the storage capacity. To get an idea of just how far computers have grown, I'm typing this book on a Mac G4 laptop with an 80GB (gigabyte) hard drive. In comparison, these early computers were lucky to have just 1MB (megabyte). My current computer has more than 80,000 times the storage capacity of some of these early machines. Likewise, My G4 runs at a speed of 1.67GHz. In comparison, an old SE runs only at 8MHz. The speed and storage capacity of today's machines were unfathomable back then. Thus, these early programmers had to figure out ways to pack a lot into a little space, and they laid the foundation for all that was to come.

The proliferation and universal adoption of the MIDI protocol in the early 80s paved the way for a plethora of computer-based software applications for the music studio. Of these, the most important was the software MIDI sequencer. The software sequencer allowed music to be recorded, edited, stored, and played back through a MIDI interface. This opened up a world of opportunities for the recording musician. Before, musicians had to record a performance as audio, committing it to analog tape, and if a mistake was made, the entire performance would have to be re-recorded. Editing was also an option, but it was a painstaking process and certainly didn't enable anyone to make changes to their melodies smoothly.

The synthesizer has two main elements: a keyboard and a sound-generating device. Nowadays, they are combined into one unit, but there was a time when they were often separate physical units. Sometimes there would be a number of different subsystems, all receiving control voltage from the same keyboard. The major breakthrough occurred when a computer running a software MIDI sequencer was inserted between the keyboard and the sound-generating device. The performance could now be recorded into a piano roll–style notation editor, where it could be stored and edited. This opened up many exciting possibilities. Software MIDI sequencers even allowed you to actually compose directly in the sequencer without even utilizing a keyboard, which was great news for composers who lacked basic keyboard chops. It also completely revolutionized the recording process, as now you could rescue almost any take without having to re-record the entire thing.

The Atari home computer opened up the door for computer-based sequencing. MIDI-based applications, such as Atari Cubase (see Figure 1.7) and Atari Notator (see Figure 1.8), were developed for the Atari system; these evolved into today's Cubase and Logic.

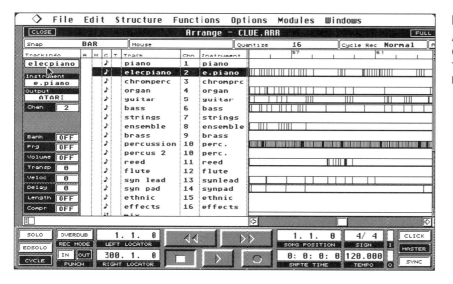

Figure 1.7

Atari Cubase
(screenshot courtesy of
Tim's Atari MIDI World:
http://tamw.atari-users.net)

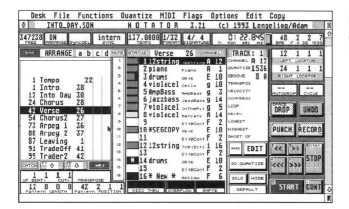

Figure 1.8

Atari Notator (screenshot courtesy of Tim's Atari MIDI World: http://tamw.atari-users.net)

Most software MIDI sequencers generally have the following basic capabilities:

- Assign MIDI channels to individual tracks of the sequence.
- Assign MIDI data in each individual track to individual instruments.
- Support at least 16 different tracks.
- Record note data in real-time to each individual track using a MIDI controller keyboard.
- Play back the MIDI data.
- Enter notes directly into the piano-roll editor.
- Edit (i.e., move, cut, copy, delete, and transpose) the data once it is in the sequencer.
- Quantize a selection of notes.
- Apply randomness to a selection of MIDI notes.
- Record velocity, pitch bend and modulation wheel data.
- Import and export standard MIDI files.
- Mix the track levels together (volume, pan).

Reason and the Evolution of the Sequencer

Reason represents a significant evolution in the development of the sequencer by combining it with powerful virtual synthesis, resulting in an incredible piece of music-creation software. To understand better the evolution of Reason, let's start by looking at Propellerheads' first application: ReBirth.

ReBirth

In 1997, Propellerhead Software released the ReBirth RB-338 (see Figure 1.9), a revolutionary software simulation of the classic Roland TR-808 and TR-909 Rhythm Composers and the TB-303 BassLine synthesizer. The original hardware units had long been discontinued, and this incredible simulation was faithful to its analog counterparts.

Figure 1.9
ReBirth RB-338.

ReBirth was met with critical acclaim, and it paved the way for things to come—setting an important precedent for the music software industry. ReBirth pioneered a new type of virtual instrument: a single piece of software that featured modeled analog synthesis, percussion synthesis, and pattern-based sequencing, all in one complete package. Propellerhead built on the success of its ReBirth application, channeling that momentum into the company's ultimate creation: Reason.

Reason

Reason represents a major evolution for the MIDI sequencer. It is a music-composition application that was conceived, developed, and released by Propellerhead Software in 2000, featuring both MIDI sequencing and software synthesis. Reason allows you to produce, sequence, mix, and master your music in a completely self-contained application within the computer. Reason's large selection of virtual instruments, real-time effects, and mastering tools make it an incredibly valuable tool for every style of music.

Software MIDI sequencers evolved to become very different from their hardware ancestors. They are loaded with many more features, and resemble their predecessors in name alone. Reason's Matrix pattern sequencer device does in fact resemble the old voltage-controlled analog hardware sequencers (see Figure 1.10). Although it has more features and flexibility than its predecessors, it does operate in a similar fashion, with its step-programmable nature and control-voltage outputs on the back.

Figure 1.10
The Reason Matrix
pattern sequencer.

The Song-Building Process

Reason took sequencing to a whole new level by combining a sequencer with powerful virtual instruments and infinite modular possibilities. The various instruments and sound modules available in Reason make it possible to sequence all the different parts of an entire song. Let's take a brief introductory look at the various parts that comprise a song and discuss a standard approach to crafting a piece of music.

There are no rules for composing or producing— no right or wrong way of approaching the process of writing a song. You can start with drums, start with a melody, start with sound design— it is all completely subjective. Wherever the inspiration strikes is the best place to start. The quality of the end result is what is important. All that really matters is that you can find a methodology that works for you. You want to find a process that maintains a certain level of organization, yet allows you enough space to be creative. Creating music should not be a struggle. It should be an enjoyable process of creative outpouring. Freedom. There's something very profound about the musical-creation process; it's about actualizing ideas and making choices. The choice of how to express yourself is yours.

Creating music involves making a series of choices. You make choices for the sound of each of the drums that make up your drum track, their relative volume levels and their L/R pan position. You choose the tempo, the key, and the overall structure of the song. Every musician, songwriter, and sound designer makes choices in the composition and arrangement of a piece of music. In the end, your music tells a story based on the choices you have made.

When you approach the creation of a piece of music, you are presented with a clean slate, blank canvas awaiting your brush strokes. Where to begin? Maybe you have an end goal in mind; maybe you will explore with no predetermined path. Both methods are completely valid for creating a piece of work that is beautiful and meaningful. The key is to figure out an approach that suits the way *you* like to work. Maybe you like to improvise and experiment. With Reason, it is easy to go back and edit an improvisation session, deleting the parts that don't work, keeping those that do. You can then take the parts that do work, get some copy-and-paste action going, and arrange your recording into a structured piece.

Sometimes you might explore an idea and get deeper and deeper, investing a lot of time into following through a particular train of thought, seeing where it leads, only to realize that it leads to nowhere, yielding no useful results. Sometimes you have to know when to say when and back all the way out. Other times, this level of detailed investigation can lead you out the other side with something extraordinary. There are choices to be made, but you have to start somewhere.

With Reason, you step up to the void with an incredible set of tools. At your disposal are powerful virtual instruments: synths, samplers, loop players, and drum machines. There are also mixers and effects, the Matrix pattern sequencer, and more. The key is having a strong working knowledge of your tools so that the actual act of using them doesn't get in the way of your creativity. It is similar to playing an instrument. You need to practice enough to keep your chops up so you can be free to explore the ideas in your head without stumbling over yourself trying to find the right notes and proper fingering.

You will find that with an improved knowledge of your tools, you will be able to reach your musical objectives more quickly and enjoyably. The less time it takes you to actualize your ideas, the more ideas you can actually explore. Once you have a fluid working knowledge of the sequencer tools, you can focus all your energy on your compositions, melodies, and musical ideas. You will find it a much more pleasurable experience as well, and so it should be.

In this book, you will examine the detailed workings of the Reason sequencer while simultaneously going through the process of producing a complete song. The following order is just one way of approaching the process of building a song, but it reflects a fairly standard approach in the industry. Remember, this is just a guideline; your own unique approach is what will give your music character and that personal touch.

Drums

For most types of popular music, the drums form the basic foundation of the song. They form the skeletal framework upon which the rest of the song is built. A tight drum beat can hold a song together. The drums can be used to accent a point, give a song movement, pick up or slow down the pace. Generally, you want to get a tight beat down and then build up from there.

There are two main methods for making beats in Reason. There is the Dr. Rex Loop Player, which plays a sampled loop known as a REX file. There's also the Redrum Drum Computer, which allows you to program your own beat with sounds of your own choosing, whether it be one of Reason's preset drum kits or a customized kit loaded up with your own WAV or AIF files. These devices can be used together or individually to create dynamic drum parts, as you will explore in Chapter 5, "Sequencing Beats in Reason."

Bass

After getting a solid drum beat down, producers usually commit the bass part to the track next. The bass rounds out the rhythm section, which is the glue that holds the whole track together. The bass is the thing that moves a track along, gives it warmth and fills the room. The bass line gets the people dancing. There are a number of different ways to create bass lines in Reason, whether you are playing them in or drawing them in. There are a variety of devices that offer great bass sounds in Reason, including the SubTractor, the Malström, the NN-19, the NN-XT, and the Combinator. You can also choose bass-line loops in the Dr REX player, or load individual bass hits into the Redrum and step-program your bass parts.

Lead

The lead melody is the element of a song that grabs your listeners and lures them in. It is what they will hopefully walk away with humming in their head. A good pop song has a solid hook, a catchy musical passage. You may want your lead melody to be charged with emotion, in which case you wouldn't want it stiff or rigid. In this case, you'd be best off leaving record quantization turned off so you can fully capture the feel of the performance. There will be times, however, when you are going for something tighter, perhaps more rigid or robotic, in which case you might want to leave the record quantization turned on. You can always record the part with input quantization turned off, and then quantize the audio after you have recorded it. You will thoroughly explore Reason's quantization features in Chapter 8, "Quantization."

Pads

A *pad* is a sound that produces a soft, imperceptible harmonic background. Pad sounds are generally rich, wide, and textured. There are string pads, warm pads, choir pads, evolving pads, and so on. In the chorus of a song, a carefully placed pad can lift the energy and induce a euphoric feeling. It is the sweetener that brings the point home. Reason has some fantastic default pad sounds to work with, and they serve as a great launching point for creating your own sounds. A strong piece of sound design is often the cornerstone of a piece of electronic music. There are also ways to create complex, evolving pads through controller automation and creative CV wiring.

Sequencing in Reason

Reason is used by songwriters, sound designers, hip-hop producers, rock bands, remix artists, film composers, and more. This chapter provides a basic overview of Reason's hardware interface, sequencer, and the powerful tools available for editing and sequencing. Reason has a number of unique features, and understanding their functionality is the best way to get the most out of this incredibly flexible application. It will also take a look at how to approach the general song-building process.

Getting Started

Before I dive into the details of working with the Reason sequencer, I want to go over a few basic concepts. If you are brand new to Reason, you definitely want to familiarize yourself with these basics before you get into the more advanced material.

Starting with an Empty Rack

The first thing you want to do when beginning a new song is to either open up an empty rack or select a pre-made template song that you have already created, loaded up with the devices you want to work with. Reason can be set to automatically open up with an empty rack every time you create a new song.

To set the default song to open up an empty rack, do the following:

1. Open the Reason menu (Mac) or the Edit menu (PC).

2. Select Preferences.

3. On the General Page, choose Empty Rack for the Default Song setting.

Starting with a Custom Default Template

You can also choose to start with a custom template that is already loaded with a basic framework that you would normally use—perhaps with some of your favorite devices along with a mixer and a mastering suite. For this exercise, we'll start off with an empty rack and then create a document that you can then use as the default template for your future productions.

To create and save a custom template and set it as the Default Song:

1. Create a new song loaded up with an empty rack (see the preceding section for help).

2. Create a Combinator MClass Mastering Suite.

3. Create a Mixer 14:2.

4. Open the File menu and save the song as DEFAULT_TEMPLATE.rns.

5. Open the Reason menu (Mac) or the Edit menu (PC).

6. Select Preferences.

7. On the General Page, choose Custom for the Default Song setting.

8. Click the folder icon to the left of the Default Song setting and browse to where you saved the file DEFAULT_TEMPLATE.rns.

When DEFAULT_TEMPLATE.rns is selected as your default song in the Preferences dialog box, Reason will automatically load this template song every time you start the program. A mixer and mastering suite will be there, ready for you to start adding instruments. You can customize this as you wish, loading it up with the tools you most often use. If you usually start off a song by programming a drum beat on the Redrum, or if you find yourself using the Digital Delay effect often, you may want to also create those devices and include them as part of your template. The key is to create a template document that best fits your style of working; doing so saves you time and keeps your workflow smooth.

At this point, open the file DEFAULT_TEMPLATE.rns and compare your document to the version on the Skill Pack CD (see Figure 2.1).

Creating a Device and Choosing a Patch

The next basic step is to create a device. The Create menu located at the top of the Reason screen lists all the various instruments, samplers, and effects available in Reason. The devices are grouped in sections. If you know what particular device you want to create, you can select it here. For example, say you want to start by programming a drum beat on the Redrum. Select Redrum Drum Computer from this list (see Figure 2.2), and the device is created and automatically routed into the first open channel on the mixer. The name of the device appears on the channel of the mixer it is routed into, and a new sequencer track is automatically created with the corresponding device name.

Figure 2.1

The default template song, including a Mixer 14:2 and an MClass Mastering Suite.

Figure 2.2

Creating a Redrum.

23

After you have created the Redrum, you can choose to load it up with your own individual sounds on each of the 10 channels or you can work with one of the preset kits. Reason comes complete with a number of individual drum and percussion one shots, along with a variety of other sounds including effects, chords, pads, and musical phrases, giving you much material to work with if you would like to build your own kits. For this example, let's load up one of the included preset drum kits.

On the lower-left corner of the Redrum device is a button with a picture of a folder on it. If you roll your mouse over it, the name of this button—Browse Patch—is revealed, as shown in Figure 2.3. Clicking this button opens a Patch Browser dialog box. On the left side of this dialog box you will see both of the main sound banks: the Reason Factory Sound Bank and the Orkester Sound Bank. Both of these sound banks contain a number of presets for the various Reason devices. The Redrum kits are located on the Reason Factory Sound Bank, so let's click that. Now you will see a list of folders containing all the various patches for each of the Reason devices. Click Redrum Drum Kits, and you will see a number of folders for various styles of music. Click Hip Hop Kits, and select Hip Hop Kit 3. This loads the Redrum's 10 channels with various hip-hop drum sounds, ready to be programmed (see Figure 2.4).

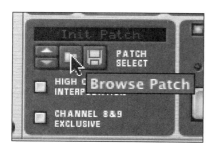

Figure 2.3

Loading a preset Redrum drum kit.

Figure 2.4

Redrum loaded with Hip Hop Kit 3.

You can also choose to create your device by browsing patches. For example, if you know you are looking for a guitar sound but you are not sure which instrument it is, you can use the Search function to find the best patch; Reason will then automatically create a new device loaded with the selected patch. To do so, do the following:

1. Open the Create menu and choose Create Device by Browsing Patches.

2. Click Reason Factory Sound Bank.

3. Type **guitar** in the search field. This returns a list of all the available guitar presets, as shown in Figure 2.5.

Figure 2.5

Use the Create Device by Browsing Patches option to find an acoustic guitar.

If you choose Ac 12 String.sxt, Reason will automatically create an NN-XT Advanced Sampler loaded with this acoustic 12-string guitar patch. This is a great feature that makes it easy to find the sound you need without having to memorize where everything is located.

Renaming a Sequencer Track

As you add devices to the sequencer, especially multiple instances of the same device, you may find it beneficial to rename the tracks so you can stay organized. For example, once you start adding multiple SubTractor devices, it becomes more difficult to keep track of which one is the bass and which one is the lead.

1. Start off by creating a SubTractor. From the Create menu, choose SubTractor.

2. Click the Browse Patch button, select Reason Factory Sound Bank, choose SubTractor Patches, click Bass, and then select Bass Guitar.

3. When you created the SubTractor, a new track was automatically created in the sequencer called SubTractor 1. Double-click the name SubTractor 1; the name becomes highlighted, letting you know that it is ready to be renamed.

4. Type **Bass** to rename SubTractor 1 to Bass.

5. Create a second SubTractor.

6. This time load the SubTractor with a lead mono-synth sound. Click the Browse Patch button, select Reason Factory Sound Bank, choose SubTractor Patches, select MonoSynths, and choose Chronic Lead.

7. A second SubTractor track has been created in the sequencer, this one called SubTractor 2. As before, double-click the name to select it, but this time type **Lead** to rename it.

You now have two different SubTractor devices in the rack, one loaded with a bass patch and the other with a lead, and both named appropriately (see Figure 2.6).

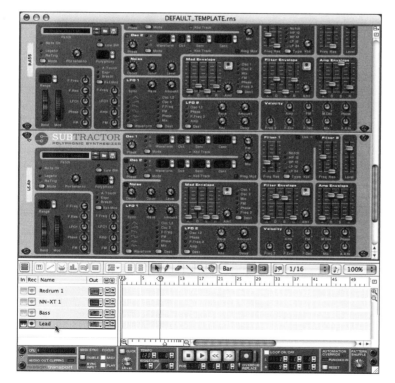

Figure 2.6

Sequencer with renamed SubTractor tracks.

Renaming the devices helps you keep better track of your instruments, and it becomes especially helpful as you add more and more devices. Note that you can also rename the track by double-clicking the little strip of tape on the corresponding mixer channel or by clicking right on the name on the device itself.

I always find it easiest to name the devices as I go along, choosing the name as I actually create them and load them up with sounds. This is the best way to keep track of which is which, because it can start to get pretty complicated once you are working with a large number of generically titled devices.

Recording Sequencer Data

There are several ways to enter MIDI data into the Reason sequencer. You can play the MIDI notes in with a MIDI keyboard controller, or you can use the Pencil tool to draw the notes directly into the appropriate lane in the sequencer. For the synths, you would draw into the Key lane; for the Redrum you would draw in the Drum lane if using the device as a sound module. A third method is to import MIDI files directly into the Reason sequencer, which I discuss in Chapter 4, "Drawing In MIDI Notes."

Playing In MIDI Notes

To record MIDI notes into the Reason sequencer, you first must arm a track for recording. Only one track at a time can receive MIDI note data from a MIDI keyboard, so first decide which instrument you want to start with. You can actually record controller data simultaneously into several tracks at once, automating filter sweeps and other types of parameter changes on several instruments at once, but the Reason sequencer only allows one track of MIDI note data to be recorded at a time. You will look at playing MIDI notes into the sequencer in full detail in Chapter 3, "Playing MIDI Notes," but I'll go over the basics of setting up a track for recording here.

To specify which track will receive incoming MIDI note data, illuminate the master keyboard MIDI input light next to the device name on the appropriate track on the left side of the sequencer by clicking it. In this instance, let's arm the Bass track for recording by clicking the Record button to the left of the word Bass so that it lights up red (see Figure 2.7).

Now that the Bass track is armed for recording, click the Global Record button in the Transport (see Figure 2.8). With the sequencer now armed for recording, clicking the Play button instructs Reason to actually begin recording incoming MIDI data into the armed track.

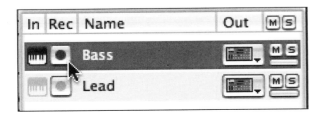

Figure 2.7
Record-enable the SubTractor Bass track.

Figure 2.8
Enable the Transport's Global Record button.

Overdub Versus Replace Mode

There are two different record modes to choose from in Reason: Overdub and Replace. The setting where you set the record mode is located directly under the Global Record button (refer to Figure 2.8). Setting the Transport control to Overdub allows you to set up a loop of a desired length and record additional layers where each pass through the loop will add the new notes to the sequencer without erasing what is already recorded. Using the Overdub mode makes sense when you are playing a very complicated part, because you can break it down into bite-size chunks, perhaps recording the left-hand melody on the first pass and the right-hand melody on the second. When recording a drum beat, you might want to start by first laying down the kick and snare, then the hi-hats and other cymbals, and finally the percussion and other sounds. This way you can focus on one or two elements with each pass as opposed to trying to play everything at once.

With the Transport's record mode set to Replace, recording data into the sequencer will actually erase anything that is already in the region where you will be recording. So, as the position pointer moves to the right, the data that was already there will be replaced by the incoming MIDI notes. If you are not actually playing any notes while you are recording in Replace mode, Reason will still delete what is already in the sequencer, replacing it with a blank slate as the position pointer moves along. Replace mode makes the most sense when punching in or correcting mistakes.

Drawing in MIDI Notes

The other way to enter MIDI data into the Reason sequencer is to actually draw the notes directly into the appropriate lane of the device you are working with. If you do not have a MIDI controller or if you prefer to draw in a more complicated melody, using Reason's Pencil tool to draw notes is a great solution. You will explore drawing in MIDI notes in full detail in Chapter 4.

Interface Overview

Reason's interface is divided into several different parts: the device rack, the sequencer, the hardware interface, and the Transport. In this section you will examine each of these different parts of the interface, familiarizing yourself with the basic layout and functioning of the software before you dive too deeply into actually sequencing MIDI.

The Hardware Interface

The Reason hardware interface is always located at the top of the rack and cannot be moved or deleted. The hardware interface consists of two parts: a MIDI IN device, where incoming MIDI data is received and routed, and the Audio OUT device, where the actual audio from Reason is routed either out the physical outputs of your audio interface or to the appropriate ReWire channel.

The MIDI IN Device

The MIDI IN device (see Figure 2.9) is used if you are controlling Reason with an external sequencer. Normally you would choose to route MIDI into the Reason sequencer by selecting the appropriate IN column, but you can also use up to four additional external MIDI inputs. This is most often used when employing Reason as a sound module when sequencing from another application or on another computer. In the Reason Preferences, on the Advanced MIDI page, you can select up to four external control busses, each one carrying 16 channels of MIDI, which can each be routed to control a different instrument in Reason. There are individual menus for each MIDI channel that list all the devices available in the current song, each channel with its own individual indicator light. When using the external control bus MIDI inputs, the incoming MIDI data on the selected bus is actually routed directly to the selected device, bypassing the Reason sequencer altogether.

Figure 2.9

The MIDI IN device.

The Audio OUT Device

Reason supports up to 64 different audio outputs in the Audio OUT device, as shown in Figure 2.10. By default, Reason has one pair of outputs. The front of the Audio OUT device has a green light for each channel, which indicates whether that channel is active. There is also a level meter that shows you if any clipping is occurring. If a particular channel is clipping, it will push the signal into the red, so you want to reduce the level for that particular audio output. By pressing the Tab key on your keyboard to flip around to the back of the Audio OUT device, you see that it is labeled Audio IN, giving you the ability to route up to 64 separate channels—or 32 stereo pairs—of audio into it.

> **Note**
> You want to avoid audio clipping; it will cause distortion and unwanted glitches in your audio.

Figure 2.10
The Audio OUT device.

The Device Rack

The upper half of the Reason interface resembles a traditional hardware rack of analog gear, except unlike a hardware rack in the real world, the Reason version is infinitely expandable, limited only by the power of your computer. As you create new devices, they are added to the hardware rack and a new track is automatically created in the sequencer.

Starting with a Mixer

I find it is helpful to begin each Reason set by first creating a Mixer 14:2 (see Figure 2.11). When you start off your session with a mixer, each subsequent device that you create is automatically routed into the next open channel on the mixer. The default template that you created earlier and shown back in Figure 2.1 incorporates both the Mixer 14:2 and Reason 3's new MClass Mastering Suite. Using a mastering suite at the end of the signal chain just before outputting the hardware outputs is a great way to get supreme sound quality out of Reason.

Figure 2.11
Starting with a MClass Mastering Suite and a Mixer 14:2.

Instruments

Once the mixer is created, it is time to build your instruments. I find it is always a good habit to click the mixer first before creating the instrument, so that the mixer is highlighted. This ensures that the new device will be auto-routed properly.

There are several types of instruments in Reason. There are the synthesizers, such as the SubTractor and Malström, samplers such as the NNXT and NN19, and drum-machine devices like the Redrum and Dr REX Loop Player. For a detailed exploration of all the features of Reason's powerful instruments, check out *Using Virtual Instruments in Reason Skill Pack* by Matt Piper (Course Technology, 2006).

These instruments each correspond to a particular lane in the Reason sequencer. The Key lane is used when sequencing the synthesizer and sampler instruments, the Drum lane for the Redrum, and the REX lane for the Dr REX. You'll take a closer look at the various lanes later in this chapter.

Effects

There are two ways to incorporate effects in Reason. You can create them as insert effects or as send effects. An *insert effect* is an effect that is literally inserted between the instrument and the mixer. Typically, compression, phasing, and distortion effects are used as insert effects. A *send effect* gets connected to an auxiliary return channel on the mixer so that several channels of audio can be sent to it at the same time. Delays and reverbs are most often used as send effects. When you create a delay or a reverb effect with a mixer already in the rack, Reason automatically routes the effect into the next open auxiliary return channel on the mixer.

Starting with the default template you created earlier, let's click the mixer and then create a DDL-1 Digital Delay Line effect by selecting it from the Create menu. Because the mixer does not have any effects yet, the delay is automatically created and routed to the first aux channel. The top red Aux knob on each of the mixer channels now routes the incoming audio signal on that channel to the delay effect. The four knobs on the far right of the mixer control the overall level of each of the connected effects. Figure 2.12 shows a Mixer 14:2 routed into the MClass Mastering Suite, with a DDL-1 Digital Delay Line effect connected to the mixer as a send effect.

If you first click an instrument in the rack and then choose to create an effect, the effect will actually be added as an insert effect. The audio output from the instrument first gets routed through the effect and then into the channel on the mixer. Thus the effect is inserted between the instrument and the mixer. This is the standard way to add a compressor effect, because you want all the audio to get routed through the compressor.

Figure 2.12

The Mixer 14:2 with a DDL-1 Digital Delay Line as a send effect.

> **Note**
>
> When you are routing audio through an insert effect, you only hear the wet output. The reverbs have a dry/wet control so you can adjust the ratio when using the effect as an insert. Reverbs work well as both insert and send effects. If you are using an effect as a send effect, it is usually a good idea to have it set to 100-percent wet and then control the dry/wet ratio by adjusting the level of the appropriate aux send knob.

The Transport

The Reason Transport features standard playback controls for the sequencer along with a metronome, tempo and time signature controls, left and right locator points, and more. This section takes a quick look at the function of the Reason Transport, giving a basic overview of the controls.

> **Note**
>
> In addition to the controls discussed here, the Transport has a Global Pattern Shuffle control, which you will look at in Chapter 8, "Quantization," and an Automation Override Reset button, which you will explore in Chapter 7, "Recording and Editing Velocity and Controller Data."

The Transport Controls

The main Transport controls function just like those on an analog tape machine. There are buttons for stop, play, rewind, fast forward, and record (see Figure 2.13). Clicking the Play button starts playback of the Reason sequencer or, if the Record button is enabled, clicking Play will begin recording data into the sequencer. Clicking Stop once stops the playback or recording of the sequencer. Clicking Stop a second time moves the position to the left locator point (assuming the current position was further along in the song than the left locator point). Clicking Stop a third time resets the position to the very beginning of the song.

Figure 2.13
The Transport controls.

Each of these controls has a corresponding computer keyboard shortcut assigned to it:

- The keyboard shortcut for Play is the Enter key on the numeric keypad.

- The spacebar toggles between Play and Stop.

- Rewind is mapped to the 7 key on the numeric keypad.

- Fast-forward is mapped to the 8 key on the numeric keypad.

- The keyboard shortcut for Stop is the 0 key on the numeric keypad or the Return key.

The Metronome

The Transport contains the Click function, with an on/off switch and an adjustable volume control (see Figure 2.14). When the Click function is activated, it plays during both recording and playback. The tempo and time signature of the Click function is determined by the song tempo, and it plays back with an accent on the first downbeat of each bar.

Figure 2.14
The Click feature.

Tempo and Signature

Next to the Click setting are the song's Tempo and Signature controls, shown in Figure 2.15. The Tempo's left field is where you set the beats per minute (bpm), while the right field allows you to make adjustments in steps of 1/1000 bpm. The Signature controls default to 4/4, adjustable with the spin controls to the right of each display. The value of the numerator counts the number of beats per bar while the value of the denominator dictates the length of each beat.

Figure 2.15

The Tempo and Signature controls.

Song Position

Underneath the playback controls in the Transport is the song position (see Figure 2.16), displayed in bars, beats, and 16th notes and corresponding to the location of the Position marker (P) along the top of the sequencer. You can change the song position by clicking the up and down arrows next to each display, or you can click and hold down your mouse button while rolling up or down. You can also double-click the display and type a position value in the format bars/beats/16th notes and then press Return. If you do not type all three values, it will automatically set the remaining numbers to their lowest value; for example, pressing 9 brings you to position 9.1.1.

Figure 2.16

Song position.

Left and Right Locator Points

To the right of the Transport playback controls are the left (L) and right (R) locator points (see Figure 2.17). These locations determine the area that will be looped when the Loop On/Off button is activated. Like the Song Position values, these values are displayed in bar/beat/16th note format, and you can similarly change the values with the spin controls to the right of each field or by double-clicking on the value and typing a new one.

Figure 2.17

The left and right locator points.

Now It's Your Turn!

To get some practice with these, set some locator points for your song and turn on the metronome to keep time when you are recording.

1. Starting with the default template you created earlier, add a SubTractor and choose the Bass Guitar sound.

2. Suppose you are planning to record an eight-bar loop that will begin at bar 9. This will give you eight bars to warm up, and then you will be in a loop. First, move the left locator point (L) to 9.1.1.

3. Because you want to record an eight-bar loop, set the right locator point (R) to 17.1.1.

4. Make sure the SubTractor track is record-enabled in the sequencer.

5. Activate the Click feature in the Transport.

6. Click the Global Record button.

If you have successfully done all these things, your song should look like the one in Figure 2.18.

Figure 2.18

Recording an eight-bar loop of a SubTractor bass guitar sound with the Click feature activated.

The Toolbar

Across the top of the sequencer is the toolbar, featuring selectable icons for all the various tools available in Reason. I briefly introduce them here, but I'll go into much more detail about them throughout the rest of the book. Indeed, the core of this book is learning how to master these tools.

The Pointer Tool

The Pointer Tool (see Figure 2.19) allows you to select notes or groups of notes and move them around. For example, say you want to extend a verse by another four bars; first, however, you'll need to move the chorus back by four bars. To do so, simply use the Pointer tool to grab all the elements and slide them back. You can select an individual note in the Key lane, or you can hold down the mouse to draw a rectangle around a group of notes to highlight all of them. Then you click and drag the mouse to move them to the desired position. You can also use the Pointer tool to resize notes. If you click a note to select it, a small black square handle appears on the right edge. You can then click this handle and drag it to make the note shorter or longer. The size of the note will be constrained by the amount selected in the Snap Value menu located in the toolbar. (The Snap to Grid function is discussed in more detail in Chapter 4, "Drawing In MIDI Notes," and Chapter 6, "Editing MIDI Notes.")

Figure 2.19
The Pointer tool.

The Pencil Tool

The Pencil tool (see Figure 2.20) lets you draw notes of a desired length. The length of the note will be constrained by the value selected in the Snap Value menu. Drawing notes makes sense when you are dealing with a complicated melody, or if you are filling in the gaps on a previous performance or correcting mistakes. The Pencil tool also lets you group a cluster of notes together in the Arrange mode, which you'll explore in more detail later in this chapter, making it easier to move a melody around or copy it and bring it in again later in the song.

Figure 2.20
The Pencil tool.

The Eraser Tool

The Eraser tool (see Figure 2.21) is used to delete events and groups in the Arrange mode. In the Edit mode, which you will explore in more detail later in this chapter, you can use the Eraser tool to delete specific notes, controller info, and pattern-change sections. You can either click individual notes or events with the Eraser tool, or hold down the mouse and draw a rectangle around several different items to delete them all at once.

Figure 2.21
The Eraser tool.

The Line Tool

The Line tool (see Figure 2.22) is useful for creating linear velocity ramp-ups and controller curves. For example, you can use the Line tool to create drum rolls by drawing in a velocity ramp-up on a successive cluster of snare hits. The Line tool gives you the ability to create a sweeping filter sound on a synth by drawing in a slowly increasing or decreasing controller curve for the filter cutoff.

Figure 2.22
The Line tool.

The Magnify Tool

The Magnify tool (see Figure 2.23) allows you to zoom in and out on the sequencer data. Zooming in is quite useful when you have recorded a passage with a cluster of notes closely spaced together and you need to get in there and fine-tune the performance—for example, making subtle edits and slightly adjusting the starting position of some of the notes. Clicking one click at a time zooms in step by step. You can also hold the mouse down to draw a box around a group of data and enlarge the entire area. Holding down Option (Mac) or Ctrl (Windows) and clicking lets you zoom out.

Figure 2.23
The Magnify tool.

The Hand Tool

The Hand tool, shown in Figure 2.24, is used to scroll the viewing area of the sequencer in one direction or another. Just select the Hand tool, click anywhere in the sequencer, hold down the mouse button, and drag in the desired direction. This comes in handy as you are editing a long series of notes and you are zoomed in tightly on those notes. You can use the Hand tool to help you quickly navigate through the material you are working with.

Figure 2.24
The Hand tool.

The Snap to Grid Function

Next to the icon for the Hand tool is a menu for selecting the snap value and a magnet icon for turning the Snap feature on or off (see Figure 2.25). When you select and edit material in both the Edit and Arrange views, the Snap function constrains the note values to a grid whose width is determined by the value selected in the Snap Value menu. For example, when drawing in notes, if the Snap Value setting is set to Bar, you will only be able to draw in notes that are at least one bar in length. You can draw in notes at some multiple of this value as well, such as notes of two-bar length, three-bar, and so on, but nothing smaller than one bar.

Figure 2.25
Snap to Grid

The Snap Value setting also affects where notes will be placed when moving data around. If you have the Snap Value set to 1/4, you will only be able to move data around to quarter-note detail. Maybe you are programming a simple four on the floor beat and you only want to have your kick drums hitting on the beats. In this case, you would adjust the Snap Value setting to 1/4. I usually set the Snap Value setting to 1/16 when I'm editing my drum parts because this gives me a little bit more flexibility, yet it still keeps everything locked in to a fairly tight grid.

Quantization Tools

On the far right along the top of the sequencer are the quantization tools, shown in Figure 2.26. These tools allow you to tighten up a recorded drum beat, correct mistakes, or alter a programmed beat to give it a different feel. Quantization involves moving recorded notes to exact note positions or closer to exact positions by a certain percentage. Reason allows you to quantize a selected group of notes, or you can use the Quantize Notes While Recording feature if you would like the incoming data to be quantized while you are playing it in. I will cover the quantization tools in depth in Chapter 8.

Figure 2.26
Quantization tools.

The Sequencer

Reason's MIDI sequencer allows you to record and edit a musical performance. The sequencer is where you build and arrange your song. When you create a new device in the Reason rack, a new sequencer track is automatically created and given the name of the new device by default. A time-line along the top of the sequencer, called the Measure ruler, displays the song position in bars and beats. The track list is on the left half of the sequencer, and the right half is where each track's corresponding MIDI data is displayed and edited. The right side is the main body of the sequencer and has two main modes: Arrange mode and Edit mode.

The Measure Ruler

As mentioned, a timeline runs along the top of the sequencer, displaying the song position in bars and beats. This is the Measure ruler, shown in Figure 2.27. The Measure ruler reads from left to right, and there is a position (P) locator point that denotes the current song position at any moment.

There are also left (L) and right (R) locator points for setting loop points or inserting and deleting bars. There is also an end (E) locator point that marks the end of the song. The Measure ruler is your reference point when composing and arranging in Reason. It serves as your timeline.

Figure 2.27
The Measure ruler.

Inserting and Removing Bars in Arrange Mode

When addressing the overall structure of your song, you will often need to rearrange the order of certain parts. Sometimes you will have to extend the length of a particular section or decrease the length of another. Suppose, for example, you want to make the chorus eight bars longer. If you have already committed data to the sequencer after the current end of the chorus, one way to achieve this would be to highlight everything in the sequencer to the right of the end of the chorus and move the highlighted bit eight bars to the right. Highlighting everything can get complicated, however, if you have a long song or a lot of tracks in the sequencer. An easier way to do this would be to simply use the Insert Bars Between Locators function to insert eight bars at the desired spot.

To practice, open the INSERTBARS.rns song file found on the CD-ROM that came with this book. Here you see a simple techno song with five different tracks in the sequencer, programmed with 64 bars of data. For the sake of example, say you want to insert eight additional bars so you can further extend the section that currently stretches from bar 33 to bar 49. To do so, set the left locator point (L) at the current end of this section at bar 49, as shown in Figure 2.28. Next, move the right locator marker (R) to bar 57. Then open the Edit menu and choose select Insert Bars Between Locators to insert eight bars beginning at bar 49; your sequence should look like the one in Figure 2.29.

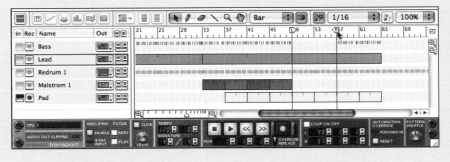

Figure 2.28
Setting the (L) and (R) locator points to insert eight bars.

39

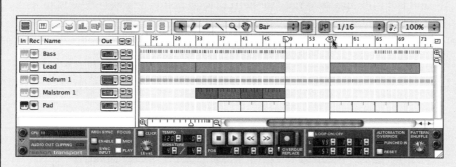

Figure 2.29

The sequencer after the eight bars have been inserted.

To remove bars from your arrangement, you follow a similar procedure. Set the left and right locator points to the appropriate positions on either side of the section you want to remove, and then select Remove Bars Between Locators from the Edit menu. Everything between the L and R locator points will be deleted, and everything to the right of the R locator point will shift to the left.

The Track List

The left side of the sequencer contains the track list (see Figure 2.30), which is divided into several columns:

- There is a column with the name of the device for that particular track of data.

- New to Reason 3, the far-right column allows you to solo or mute a particular track directly from the sequencer.

- To the left of the device name is a column in which you select the device that will receive incoming note data from your MIDI controller. Only one device at a time can record incoming MIDI note data, which is determined by the keyboard icon in the far-left column of the track.

Note

There are ways in Reason to set up several different MIDI keyboards to play different instruments—for example, for a live-performance situation—but for the purpose of committing a performance to the sequencer, you can only record MIDI note data into one track at a time. You can, however, record multiple parameter automations on several devices at once, which I'll get into in Chapter 7.

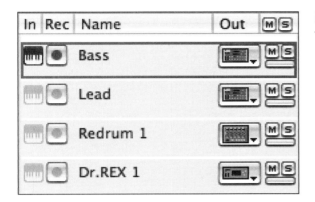

Figure 2.30
The track list.

Sequencer Views

The Reason sequencer has two distinct ways of viewing information: the Edit mode and the Arrange mode. A button in the upper-left corner of the sequencer lets you toggle between the two views. In Arrange mode, the icon appears as three colored lines—red, blue, and yellow—indicative of the various lanes shown in the Edit mode. In Edit mode, the icon appears to feature groups of data, as you would see in the Arrange mode (see Figure 2.31). Clicking this icon toggles back and forth between the two views. You can also toggle between Arrange mode and Edit mode by pressing Shift+Tab or Command/Ctrl+E.

Figure 2.31
The Switch to Edit Mode and Switch to Arrange Mode toggle buttons.

The Arrange Mode

The Arrange mode (see Figure 2.32) gives you an overview of all the tracks, showing multiple tracks of data at once. This mode offers you an overall sense of the arrangement, so you can look at how the different parts of the song will play against each other. The Arrange mode is best suited for working out the bigger picture of your song, copying and pasting across several tracks, moving around groups of data, and generally deciding how you wish to arrange your song. You can also highlight several tracks of data to apply quantization to all of them at once, as you will see in Chapter 8. In addition, you can insert and remove bars in the Arrange mode.

Exploring the Sequencer Track

In the Arrange mode, each sequencer track is divided into three different sections or lanes, where events are displayed as vertical lines (see Figure 2.33). The top lane, a white lane, is where note, drum, and REX data are displayed as red vertical lines. No distinction is made in the Arrange mode between notes of different pitch. Every note appears as the same vertical red line regardless of its pitch to give you a sense of when the notes are actually triggered.

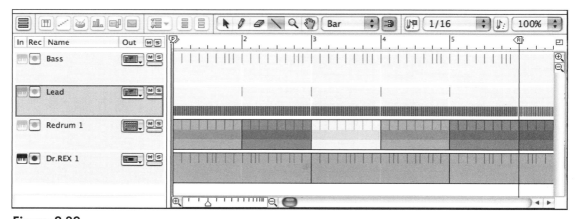

Figure 2.32

The sequencer's Arrange mode.

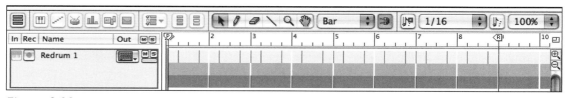

Figure 2.33

The sequencer track with automation data in all three lanes.

If a particular sequencer track has no pattern changes and there are no automated parameters in the Controller lane, it will appear white throughout. However, if a particular track *does* features pattern-change data, then the middle third of that track will appear yellow in the Arrange mode. Vertical lines indicate where each pattern change occurs. The bottom third of each sequencer track will appear blue if any of the device's controller-value parameters are automated.

Working with Groups in the Arrange Mode

You may find it helpful at times to work with a series of events as one unit. In Reason, you can take a selection of events and treat it as one unit called a *group*. The Arrange mode is the place where you create these groups of data. For example, suppose you have an eight-bar melody that you want to repeat several times. Using the Pencil tool, you can draw a rectangle around all the notes in that bar to group them together as one single unit. This group can then be copied to other parts of your song; they can also be moved, resized, divided, combined, and deleted. As shown in Figure 2.34, groups appear as colored boxes—all the boxes that are the same color contain the same event data. Chapter 6 discusses the creation of groups in detail.

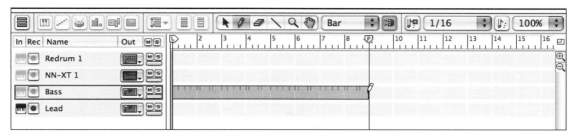

Figure 2.34
Creating groups in the Arrange mode with the Pencil tool.

The Edit Mode

The Edit mode (see Figure 2.35), which lets you see all the data for one device at a time, is where you can make detailed edits to a particular track. This includes drawing, erasing, or moving around notes, adjusting the velocity and controller parameters, as well as automating pattern changes. When working in the Edit mode, clicking the different track names reveals the related MIDI data for that particular device.

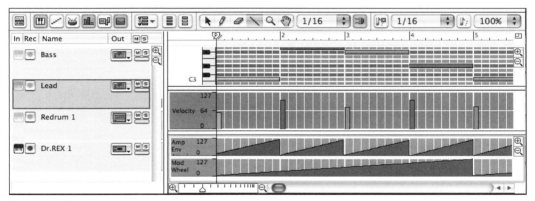

Figure 2.35
The sequencer's Edit mode.

The Edit mode is divided vertically into rows called *lanes*. There are six different lanes for editing different types of data:

■ **The Key lane.** This lane—which resembles a piano roll, featuring the black and white keys of the keyboard stretching vertically on the left side with a corresponding dark blue and light blue background (see Figure 2.36)—is where you enter your notes, either by drawing them in or by playing them with a MIDI keyboard. This lane spans the entire MIDI note range, from C-2 to G8, and is used with the SubTractor, Malström, NN19, and NN-XT, as well as with certain Combinator patches that include one or more of these devices.

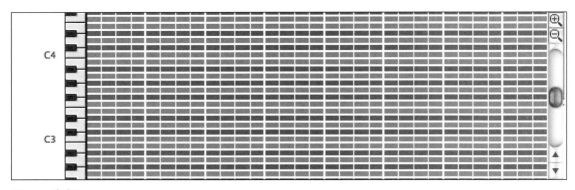

Figure 2.36

The Key lane.

> **Tip**
> You can click your mouse on the keyboard on the left to preview the sound. This is helpful when searching for the appropriate pitch.

■ **The REX lane.** This lane, shown in Figure 2.37, is vertically divided into pitches from C3 on up, which correspond to all the slices that make up a particular REX loop. The REX lane is similar to the Key lane in that you can click the different slices to preview each one. When you click the To Track button on the Dr REX Loop Player, it prints the information into the REX lane. In the lane, the actual notes are shown as boxes. The width of each box signifies the length of the associated note, and the box's color indicates the note's velocity. (Darker colors indicate a higher velocity.)

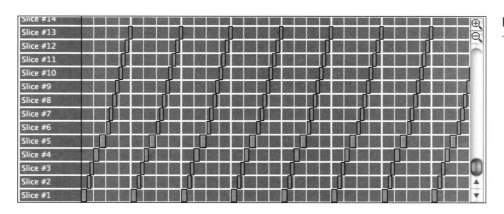

Figure 2.37

The REX lane.

■ **The Drum lane.** The Drum lane (see Figure 2.38), which is used to edit drum tracks, is divided into 10 sections that correspond to the 10 channels on the Redrum drum computer. Each channel is named after the sample that is loaded into it. Like the Key and REX lanes, you can click the sample names on the left vertical column to preview the sounds.

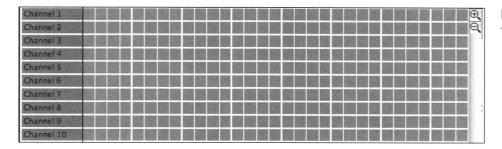

Figure 2.38
The Drum lane.

■ **The Velocity lane.** This lane, shown in Figure 2.39, is where you edit the velocity values of the notes on that particular track in the sequencer. The velocity value of each note, which can range from 0–127, is shown as a vertical bar, with taller bars indicating a higher velocity. The velocity is color coded as well; the taller notes are also darker in color, reflecting a higher velocity.

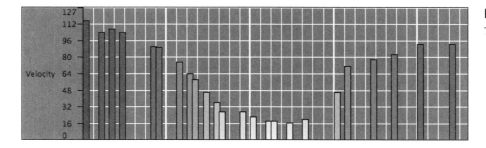

Figure 2.39
The Velocity lane.

Tip

You can use the Pencil tool to edit the velocity, drawing changes right into the Velocity lane. To do so, click and hold on a bar and drag up or down to increase or decrease the velocity. You can also click directly above a bar to make the value immediately jump to the mouse position. The Line tool works great for drawing in linear increases—for example, to create a drum roll.

■ **The Pattern lane.** The yellow Pattern lane, shown in Figure 2.40, is the lane in which you view and edit automation for pattern-based devices like the Redrum and the Matrix. You can program up to 32 different drum patterns on the Redrum, and then use the tools in the Pattern lane to specify when the various patterns will play. You can create different patterns for the different sections of your song—the intro, verse, chorus, fills, and so on; click the triangle on the left side to select the pattern, and then use the Pencil tool to draw a stretch of time when you want that pattern to play. The pattern change shows up on a little tab with the bank and pattern number and stretches to the right as long as that selected pattern is active, which it will be until the next pattern is selected.

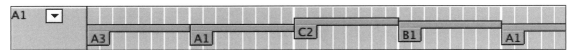

Figure 2.40
The Pattern lane.

■ **The Controller lane.** This lane automates the various parameters of each of the different instruments. The blue Controller lane (see Figure 2.41) is where you view and edit parameter automation for specific parameters of a particular device. Each sequencer track has a number of Controller lane subtracks, one for each parameter that can be automated. You can automate the pan position for a particular drum sound on a Redrum or automate a filter on a synth to create a sweeping effect. If you haven't yet recorded any automation for a particular parameter, it appears blank in the Controller lane. Once you record automation for that parameter at any point in the song, the entire track gets filled up with data, maintaining a static value for the rest of the song based on the controller's original position when you first started recording. You can then go in with the Pencil or Line tool and draw in automation curves for the rest of the song.

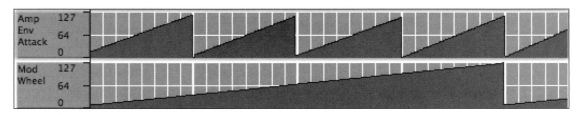

Figure 2.41
The Controller lane.

Why Can't I See All the Lanes?

By default, the lanes that appear in the Edit mode are determined by the device to which that particular track is connected. For Dr REX tracks, the REX lane and the Velocity lane are shown. For Redrum tracks, the Drum lane, Velocity lane, and Pattern lane are shown. SubTractor tracks have a Key lane and a Velocity lane, and so on. Once you show or hide lanes for a particular track, the sequencer stores that data and remembers which combination of lanes to show the next time you select that device. You'll explore the unique features of each of these lanes in more detail throughout the course of this book.

Showing and Hiding Lanes

You can choose to show or hide the lanes of data in the Edit mode by clicking their associated icons in the toolbar along the top of the sequencer, as shown in Figure 2.42. Reason also has a handy roll-over feature so that if you hover your mouse over an icon, the icon's name is revealed. This is a helpful feature if you are unclear of the function of a particular icon.

Figure 2.42
Buttons to show/hide lanes.

Tip

Hiding lanes makes sense if you need more room to work. If you hold down the Option (Mac) or Alt (Windows) key and click a lane button, only that lane will be shown; all other lanes will be hidden.

Resizing and Zooming Lanes

When working in the Edit mode, each lane can be adjusted to give you more or less viewing area. Being able to customize the size of the viewing area is quite helpful, especially when you are doing some detailed editing. To change the size of a lane, hover your mouse above the horizontal divider that separates the lanes. The mouse changes from a pointer into an icon with up/down arrows; click and drag the divider up or down to change its size as I have in Figure 2.43. In addition, you can change the size of certain lanes—namely, the Key, REX, Drum, and Controller lanes—by using their zoom functions, which are accessible from the pairs of magnifying glasses in each lane's upper-right corner. Clicking the magnifying glass with the plus sign zooms in, and clicking the one with the minus sign zooms out.

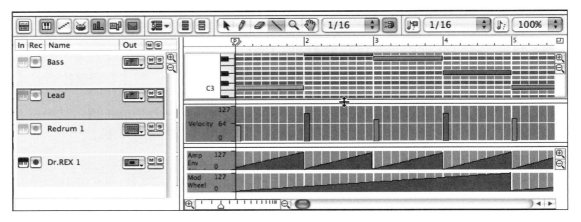

Figure 2.43

The cursor changes into one with up/down arrows, enabling you to adjust the viewing area of the Velocity lane.

Now It's Your Turn!

Okay, let's run through a little exercise to get familiar with the different lanes in the Edit mode. Do the following:

1. Open the file 2_SubTractors.rns, located on the CD-ROM that accompanies this book.

2. Click the Switch to Edit Mode button in the upper-left corner of the sequencer.

3. Click the Bass track.

4. Change the Snap Value setting from 1/4 to Bar.

5. Click the Pencil tool.

6. Starting at bar one, draw four successive one bar–length notes: C3, D3, E3, and F3.

7. Grab the right locator point (R) and move it to bar five to create a four-bar loop.

8. Open the file 2SubTractorsAfter.rns, located on the CD-ROM that accompanies this book, to check your work (see Figure 2.44).

Detaching the Sequencer

If you are going to be doing a lot of editing and you have a large screen or are working with two monitors, you may find it helpful to detach the sequencer and enlarge it to fill the second monitor. To detach the sequencer, open the Window menu and select Detach Sequencer Window (see Figure 2.45) or click the Detach Sequencer button in the rack, as shown in Figure 2.46.

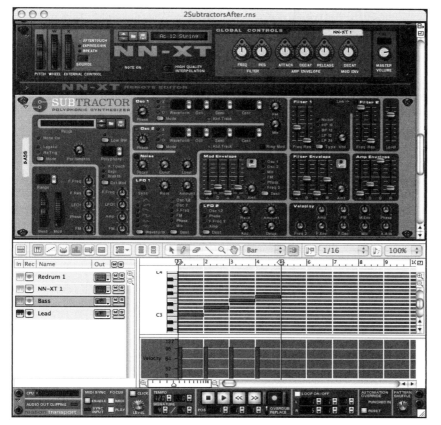

Figure 2.44
The exercise results.

Figure 2.45
Choose Detach Sequencer Window from the Window menu.

Figure 2.46
Click the Detach Sequencer Window button.

To reattach the sequencer, select open the Window menu and choose Attach Sequencer Window or click the Attach Sequencer button either in the rack or in the detached sequencer window (see Figure 2.47).

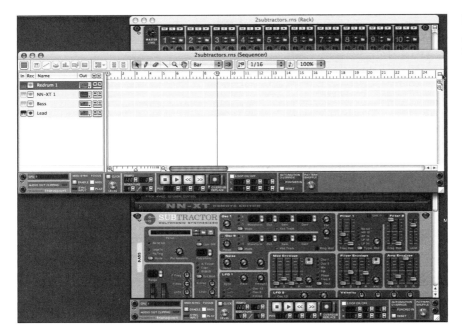

Figure 2.47

Attach Sequencer button

Maximizing the Sequencer Area

You can choose to maximize the sequencer area so that it fills up the entire Reason rack. To do so, click the Maximize Sequencer button in the upper-right corner of the sequencer window, as shown in Figure 2.48. Alternatively, you can maximize the sequencer area by holding down the Command (Mac) or Ctrl (Windows) key and pressing the number 2 on the typing keyboard.

When the sequencer is maximized, the same button that was used to maximize it can be used to minimize it (see Figure 2.49). Click this button to return the sequencer to the size it was before being maximized; once again, you'll be able to see the devices in the device rack.

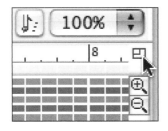

Figure 2.48

The Maximize Sequencer button.

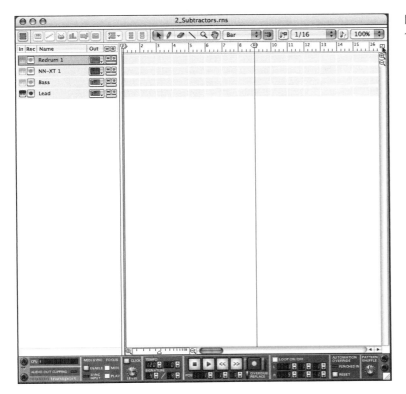

Figure 2.49

The Minimize Sequencer button

Adjusting Horizontal and Vertical Zoom

The sequencer allows you to adjust both the horizontal and vertical zoom. The controls for doing so appear as magnifying glasses with a plus and minus sign for zooming in and out, respectively. The vertical zoom controls are located in the upper-right corner of the sequencer, and the horizontal zoom controls are located along the bottom, just above the Tempo/Time Signature settings in the Transport. For the horizontal zoom, you can either click the magnifying glasses one step at a time to zoom in or out, or you can grab the slider to adjust the zoom more quickly, as shown in Figure 2.50.

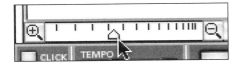

Figure 2.50

Adjusting the sequencer's horizontal zoom.

You can also use the Magnify tool in the toolbar to easily zoom in on a particular selection. When using the Magnify tool, however, you actually are zooming in both horizontally *and* vertically. If, say, you are editing a particularly dense cluster of notes and you have the vertical size of your sequencer set so it actually includes all the notes in your melody and allows you to see all the devices in the rack, you'll probably want to zoom in horizontally only and leave the vertical setting alone.

3 Playing MIDI Notes

There are several ways to input MIDI data into the sequencer in Reason. This chapter takes a look at playing in notes with a MIDI controller keyboard. First it goes over the basics of setting up Reason to properly receive MIDI input. Then it covers the details of setting up a track for recording. Finally, it examines some of the available recording options such as Overdub versus Replace mode and the Quantize Notes During Recording function.

Setting Up the Control Surface

In order to record a MIDI performance, you must first ensure that your MIDI controller is properly installed, connected, and recognized by the computer. Some devices are class compliant, meaning there is no driver to install; you just plug it into your computer and you are ready to go. Oftentimes, however, you will first need to install a driver in order to allow your controller to effectively communicate with the computer. Every manufacturer's device has its own unique features and installation requirements. You normally want to install the driver before plugging in the device, and often you will need to reboot for the installation to be complete. Most MIDI controllers are USB devices, and it is generally a good idea to plug them directly into a USB port on your computer as opposed to plugging it into a USB hub. If you encounter difficulties with the installation, refer to the instructions that were included with your MIDI controller or contact the manufacturer's tech support department for further assistance.

The Remote Protocol

Reason 3 introduced a new protocol, Remote, to handle the MIDI input from control surfaces. There is a huge variety of devices out there from which to choose, including MIDI keyboards, foot controllers, MIDI drum pads, and remote-control units with knobs, buttons, and faders. Remote helps you easily integrate your control surface with Reason. It is essentially a mapping system that offers direct, hands-on control of all the various parameters for each Reason device. Most control surfaces from all the major manufacturers are already supported, where all the knobs, faders, and buttons on the MIDI controller are automatically mapped to the most logical parameters on each particular Reason instrument.

Using Reason Preferences to Set Up Your Control Surface

To set up your control surface, do the following:

1. Select Preferences from the Reason menu (Mac) or from the Edit menu (PC), as shown in Figure 3.1.

Figure 3.1

Select the Preferences command.

2. The Preferences dialog box displays the General tab by default. Switch to the Control Surfaces tab by opening the drop-down list at the top of the dialog box and selecting Control Surfaces and Keyboards (see Figure 3.2).

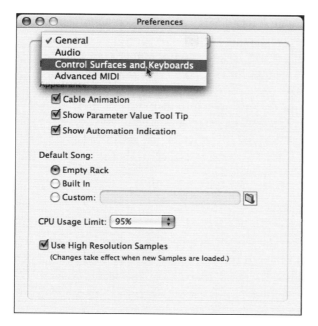

Figure 3.2

Select Control Surfaces and Keyboards from the menu at the top of the Preferences dialog box.

Reason should automatically recognize any MIDI controller or keyboard that is properly installed and connected to your computer. An Attached Surfaces window appears, showing a picture of your device, the model and manufacturer name, and whether the device has been designated as the master keyboard. It also features a green checkmark if the MIDI device is properly installed and recognized. If a device was connected previously but it is no longer available, it appears with a red ×. If you want to be able to use the connected device with Reason, ensure that the Use with Reason checkbox is checked.

Auto-Detecting the Control Surface

If you have properly installed your MIDI controller but it is not recognized by Reason, try refreshing the Control Surfaces and Keyboards tab of the Preferences dialog box by clicking the Auto-Detect Surfaces button (see Figure 3.3). Reason will rescan your ports for any connected device; if the device is detected, it will show up in the Attached Surfaces area of the dialog box.

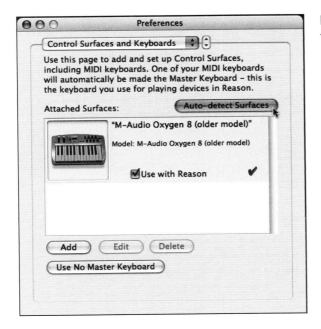

Figure 3.3

The Auto-Detect Surfaces button.

Manually Detecting the Control Surface

Not all control surfaces support auto-detection, so you may need to add the device manually if Reason does not automatically find the device. Here's how:

1. Click the Add button.

2. In the window that appears (see Figure 3.4), open the Manufacturer drop-down list and select the manufacturer of your control surface.

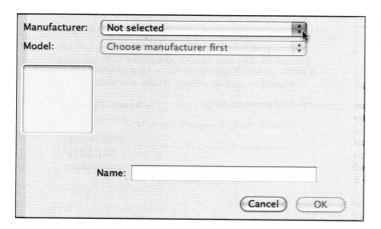

Figure 3.4

Add a control surface manually.

3. Open the Model drop-down list and choose the device model.

4. An image of the control surface will appear, along with some text with any relevant information about the device, such as which preset it should utilize for Reason. Click OK to return to the Control Surfaces page of the Preferences dialog box.

If you are using a controller that is *not* on the list, choose Other from the Manufacturer list and select the appropriate keyboard or controller type from the Model list. Alternatively, click the Find button; this launches a window that instructs you to move a control or press a key on the control surface. When you do, Reason should be able to properly identify the device.

Setting a Master Keyboard

The first control surface that features a keyboard that is added to the Control Surfaces and Keyboards list is automatically designated as the master keyboard. When you add an additional MIDI controller, you then have the option to highlight one of the devices and click the Make Master Keyboard button (see Figure 3.5). You can have only one master keyboard, although you have the ability to select which device that will be on the Attached Surfaces page. You also have the option to use no master keyboard.

Locking a Control Surface to a Device

Reason allows you to lock a control surface (other than the master keyboard) to a specific device so that the control surface will always control that particular device, regardless of which track has MIDI input in the sequencer. This allows you to play and record notes for one device while simultaneously controlling parameters on another device with a different control surface. In fact, you can lock several control surfaces to the same device in Reason. As mentioned, however, the designated master keyboard cannot be locked.

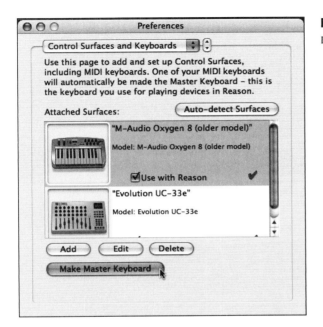

Figure 3.5

Designating a master keyboard.

To lock a control surface to a device, do the following:

1. Select Surface Locking from Reason's Options menu, as shown in Figure 3.6.

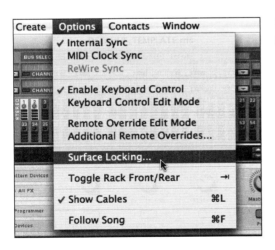

Figure 3.6

Selecting Surface Locking from the Options menu.

2. In the Surface Locking dialog box that appears, open the Surface menu to see a list of all installed control surfaces, except for the one you have designated as the master keyboard. Select the control surface you would like to lock to a device.

3. Open the Lock to Device menu to see a list of all the devices in the current song (see Figure 3.7). Choose the device you want to lock to the selected control surface. The information about which devices are locked to which control surfaces is saved with the song.

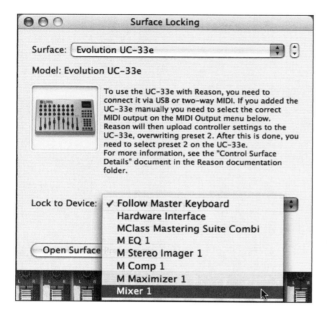

Figure 3.7
The Surface Locking dialog box.

You might utilize this control surface–locking feature if you have several MIDI controllers or keyboards. It is also very handy if you are performing live and you want to always have certain controllers controlling certain instruments. Perhaps you might have one control surface locked to the mixer so it can always control the levels of the different instruments. Perhaps you have a drum-pad controller such as the M-Audio Trigger Finger (see Figure 3.8), and you want it to always play the Redrum. Perhaps you have two keyboards and you want one to always be playing the SubTractor loaded with a bass patch, and the other to be the master keyboard, moving through a variety of instruments. There are many different ways to utilize Reason, and as you spend more and more time with it, you will discover and develop your own unique approach to taking advantage of this powerful and flexible application.

Recording a Live Performance

Now that you have your MIDI control surface properly set up in Reason, it is time to dive into the recording process. After you have created an instrument and selected a sound, you then have to arm the appropriate sequencer track for recording and enable the Global Record button. This section covers the basics of setting up a track for recording a live performance and examines some of the recording options available to you.

Figure 3.8
The M-Audio Trigger Finger.

Arming a Track for Recording

Each track in the sequencer has several columns of information on the left side including the track name, In and Out columns, and buttons for mute, solo, and record. In order to record MIDI notes into the Reason sequencer, one of the tracks must be armed for recording. You can record MIDI note information into only one track at a time. The far-left column, labeled "In," features a keyboard icon that shows which sequencer track will be receiving the MIDI note information from the designated master keyboard. The sequencer track that is set to receive input from the master keyboard MIDI input will be illuminated, while all the other tracks will appear grayed out.

The next column over is labeled "Rec," and features a square around a small circle. Clicking the circle turns it red and record-enables that particular sequencer track. Figure 3.9 shows an example of a song with both a Redrum device and a SubTractor device where the SubTractor is armed for recording and set to receive the master keyboard MIDI input.

Although you can record MIDI note information into only one track at a time, you can record controller automation data onto several tracks at once. Figure 3.10 shows the same song with the SubTractor track record enabled and set to receive the master keyboard MIDI note information; now, however, the Redrum sequencer track is also record enabled, ready to record any controller automation data for that device. You will thoroughly explore the concept of recording controller data in Chapter 7, "Recording and Editing Velocity and Controller Data."

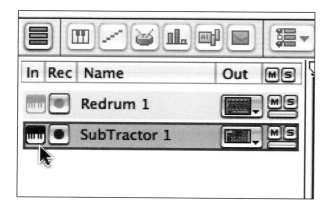

Figure 3.9

SubTractor track record enabled and designated to receive master keyboard MIDI input.

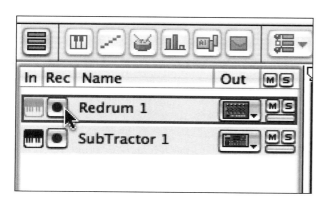

Figure 3.10

SubTractor track record enabled and designated to receive master keyboard MIDI input. Redrum track record enabled to receive controller data.

Exercise: Arming a Track for Recording

Let's do a simple exercise to ensure that you grasp these basic concepts.

1. Open the file ArmTrackBefore.rns from the included CD-ROM. You should see an MClass Mastering Suite, a Mixer 14:2, and a Redrum.

2. Click the mixer to select it.

3. Create a SubTractor by opening the Create menu and choosing SubTractor.

4. Load the Bass Guitar patch for the SubTractor by clicking the SubTractor's Browse Patch folder, selecting Reason Factory Sound Bank, choosing SubTractor Patches, selecting Bass, and clicking Bass Guitar.

5. When you create a new SubTractor device, it is automatically set to receive incoming master keyboard MIDI input. Suppose, however, that you want to record the Redrum part first. To enable this, click the master keyboard icon in the Redrum track's In column. The master keyboard icon should now be lit for the Redrum device, and the red Record button for the SubTractor sequencer track should now be turned off.

6. Suppose you wish to simultaneously record note information for the Redrum and some controller automation for the SubTractor. To do so, click the Record Enable button for the SubTractor track, but make sure you leave the Redrum device set to receive the master keyboard MIDI input.

7. Open ArmTrackAfter.rns from the included CD-ROM and check your work against it (see Figure 3.11).

Figure 3.11

A SubTractor track armed for recording controller data, with the Redrum to receive master keyboard MIDI input.

Using the Global Record Button

The Global Record button in the Reason Transport (see Figure 3.12) activates recording. The keyboard shortcut for enabling this Record button is the asterisk (*) on the numeric keypad. Alternatively, you can hold down the Command (Mac) or Ctrl (PC) key and press Return (Mac) or Enter (PC). If the song is currently stopped, hitting Play will begin recording. If Reason was already playing, clicking the Global Record button will act like a punch in. Either way, Reason will begin recording at the current song position. Clicking the Global Record button again while Reason is actually recording acts as a punch out. This is useful if you are looking to redo a certain small part of a performance, keeping the rest intact.

Figure 3.12
The Global Record button.

Overdub Mode Versus Replace Mode

There are two main recording modes in Reason: Overdub and Replace. To switch between the two modes, click the switch underneath the Global Record button in the Transport (see Figure 3.13). This section covers these two record modes and gives some examples of when you might want to use each of them.

Figure 3.13
Toggle between Overdub and Replace mode.

Overdub Mode

In Overdub mode, any newly recorded information is added to whatever was already in the sequencer. Overdub mode is what you would use for loop recording. For example, suppose you are playing a complex part. By breaking it down and recording the left hand on the first pass and the right hand on the second pass, you can actually tackle a complex piece that you might not be able to play all at once.

Overdub mode is ideal for when you want to layer different melodies across different octaves for a particular instrument. Say you have a 25 key MIDI controller such as the Oxygen 8 (Figure 3.14) and a piano patch loaded up in an NNXT and you want to record a bass line as well as melodies in several different octaves. Because you can access only two octaves at a time with your MIDI controller, the only way to record a piece with notes outside this range is to make several different passes, shifting the keyboard's octave up or down with each pass.

Figure 3.14
The Oxygen 8 MIDI controller.

Overdub mode is also ideal for recording drum parts. It allows you to focus on a few elements at a time and then build on what you already have. For example, the Redrum has 10 different channels. Although you do in fact have 10 fingers, odds are you will find it much easier to focus on just a few sounds at a time as opposed to playing all of them at once. Maybe you lay down the kick and the snare on the first pass, then add the high hats, and then revisit it again to throw down the toms and various sound effects. Overdub mode allows you to tackle a little bit at a time so that you can actually get a solid recording instead of biting off more than you can chew.

Replace Mode

When working in Replace mode, any newly recorded information will replace any previously recorded information in the sequencer. This also includes silence, so if you hit record and are in Replace mode, the position marker will move to the right across the sequencer, erasing everything in its path. For this reason, it is probably a good idea to use Overdub mode as your default recording mode, as you might want to avoid accidentally recording over any material.

Replace mode is ideal for punching in. Say you have recorded a near-perfect pass but you played a fairly uninspired part for the solo and you would like to re-record it. In a case like this, you might want to go back and just record right over your previous take since you know for sure that you do not want to use it. Although it is true that you can press Ctrl+Z (PC) or Command+Z (Mac) to perform the Undo function if you accidentally record over something you wanted to keep, there's no way to actually keep part of the new recording and part of the previous recording in Replace mode. I would strongly recommend that you use Replace mode only when you are absolutely sure you do not want to keep something already in the sequencer. Sometimes I like to copy the notes from a previous take and paste them in at the very end of the song, just in case I change my mind.

Exercise: Overdub Recording

Let's do a little exercise with the Redrum utilizing Overdub mode.

1. Start by opening the file OverdubBefore.rns on the included CD-ROM. You'll see a song loaded up with a Mixer 14:2, a SubTractor with a Bass Guitar patch, and a Redrum loaded with sounds for each of the 10 channels.

2. Let's set up to record a simple two-bar loop from bar two to bar four. This gives you a one-bar count-in. Set the left locator (L) to 2.1.1 and the right locator (R) to 4.1.1, and turn on the Loop function (see Figure 3.15).

Figure 3.15
Activate the Loop function.

3. Activate the click/metronome.

4. Click the master keyboard icon on the Redrum sequencer track so it is illuminated, and make sure the Redrum track is record enabled as well.

5. Activate the Global Record button.

6. Change the mode from Replace to Overdub.

7. The 10 Redrum channels correspond to the notes C1 to A1 on your keyboard. C1 plays the kick drum sound; C#1 plays a snare; and so on. Take a moment to familiarize yourself with which key triggers which sound.

8. Create a simple beat by adding one layer at a time each pass through the loop. The first time around, play the kick drum (C1) on the first and third beat of each measure.

9. The next time around, play the snare (C#1) on the second and fourth beat of each measure. (If you aren't able to switch over to the snare right away, you can wait until it goes around the loop again.)

10. Counting off "1 and 2 and 3 and 4 and" for each measure, add a high hat on each "and." You have just created a basic beat!

11. Check your work against the file OverdubAfter.rns on the included CD-ROM (see Figure 3.16).

Figure 3.16

A basic beat recorded for the Redrum in the Drum lane.

Using this technique, you can continue layering additional parts on top of each other to craft more and more complex rhythms. If you want to keep listening to the loop while you try out different sounds on top of it, you can click the Global Record button again to deactivate it. Reason will keep playing and you will still hear your loop; you can now practice adding the next part to the drum loop. When you are ready to commit it to the track, just hit the Global Record button to begin recording again.

> **Tip**
>
> Once I have a basic structure down, I like to turn off the click track and hear what the loop sounds like on its own. I find that I sometimes get used to hearing the metronome in there and end up building an entire beat around it, and then when I turn off the metronome the beat sounds like it's lacking. If that is the case, you can always find a click-like sound and then add it to each beat of each measure to give you the same effect, since that is essentially what the metronome is doing.

Using the Quantize Notes During Recording Function

Reason gives you the ability to actually quantize notes automatically while they are being recorded. To use this feature, click the Quantize Notes During Recording button in the toolbar just above the sequencer to the right of the magnet-shaped Snap to Grid button (see Figure 3.17). When Quantize Notes During Recording is activated, incoming notes are constrained to a grid determined by the Quantize Value and Quantize Strength settings.

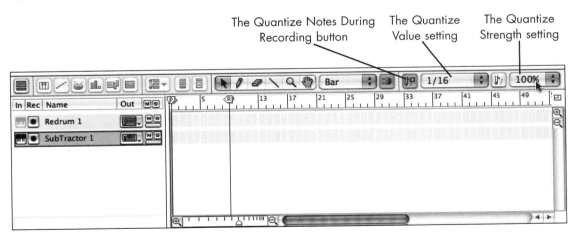

Figure 3.17
The Quantize Notes During Recording feature.

Setting the Quantize Value

The Quantize Value drop-down list has settings ranging from Bar down to 1/64 note, along with Shuffle, Groove 1, Groove 2, Groove 3, and User settings (see Figure 3.18). Setting the Quantize Value option to Bar forces any notes played to the very first beat of each measure. This is probably a bit much unless perhaps you were playing in long chords. A more practical setting for Quantize Value would be the 1/16 note setting, especially for drum recording. Setting the Quantize Value to 1/16 forces all incoming notes to or closer to the closest 1/16th note position on the grid.

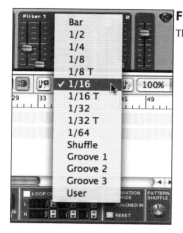

Figure 3.18

The Quantize Value drop-down list.

Using the Shuffle setting creates a swing feel. Setting the Quantize Value to Shuffle forces incoming notes towards 1/16 note positions unless you apply a different amount of shuffle, as determined by the Pattern Shuffle knob in the lower-right corner of the Transport (see Figure 3.19).

Figure 3.19

The Pattern Shuffle knob.

The Quantize Value menu also contains settings for Groove 1, Groove 2, and Groove 3, which are slightly irregular default rhythmic patterns. Selecting one of these forces the incoming notes toward the selected groove pattern, which gives it a different rhythmic feel for each one.

Finally, there is the User setting. This selection allows you to capture your own groove and apply it with the Quantize function. Say, for example, you love the feel of a particular REX file. Reason gives you the ability to extract the feel or groove of this REX loop and then apply it to another part. If you are going to be recording a drum part for a Redrum device that you have loaded up with sounds, you can first capture the feel of the REX file and then apply that as the setting for the Quantize Value. Then, incoming notes will be forced to have the same feel as your beloved REX loop, yet they will be the sounds you have selected for the Redrum. You will thoroughly explore this function in Chapter 8, "Quantization."

Setting the Quantize Strength

The Quantize Strength setting is a percentage value that governs just how much each note will be moved. If Quantize Strength is set to 100%, then all incoming notes will be forced precisely to the grid determined by the Snap Value setting. Setting Quantize Strength to 50% moves incoming notes halfway to the grid determined by the Snap Value setting, and so on.

Exercise: Quantize Notes During Recording

Let's now do an exercise to practice using the Quantize Notes During Recording function.

1. Open QuantizeNotesDuringBefore.RNS. This is a song with an MClass Mastering Suite, a Mixer 14:2, a Redrum loaded with a kit, a SubTractor loaded with a bass patch, and a Malström loaded with an evolving pad called Chilloutput.

2. Turn on the Quantize Notes During Recording feature.

3. Change the Quantize Value setting to Bar.

4. Change the Quantize Strength setting to 100%

5. Click the master keyboard icon on the Malström track.

6. Activate the Global Record button in the Transport.

7. Play the following simple eight-bar progression, playing just one note for at least a bar or two length each time. Play two bars of B, one bar of A, one bar of D, two bars of B, one bar of A, and one bar of E.

8. Open QuantizeNoteDuringAfter.RNS and check your work.

4 Drawing In MIDI Notes

The last chapter looked at inputting MIDI notes into the sequencer by recording a live performance. This chapter examines how you can use Reason's Pencil tool to draw notes directly into the sequencer. Sometimes drawing in the notes is more practical than playing them in; I often take advantage of both techniques in my own productions, depending on the situation.

Using the Pencil Tool to Draw In Notes

Reason's Pencil tool (see Figure 4.1) allows you to draw MIDI notes directly into the sequencer. You draw notes in the sequencer's Edit mode into one of three lanes: the Key lane, the Drum lane or the REX lane. After you have selected the Pencil tool, drawing in notes is simple. Just select the appropriate lane of the instrument for which you wish to draw in notes and then click the grid to draw in notes where you would like them to appear.

Figure 4.1
The Pencil tool.

Snap to Grid

Using Reason's Snap to Grid function enables you to restrict the size of the notes you are drawing and where on the measure they start. For example, say you want to only draw in notes that are 1/16 note long or a multiple of 1/16 notes. The first thing you need to do is activate the Snap to Grid function by clicking the Snap to Grid button in the toolbar (it's the one with a magnet on it, as shown in Figure 4.2). When activated, the Snap to Grid button appears highlighted in blue. Next, you want to set the Snap value to the appropriate value. In this example, let's set the Snap value to 1/16 note (see Figure 4.3).

Figure 4.2

Click this button to toggle the Snap to Grid function on and off

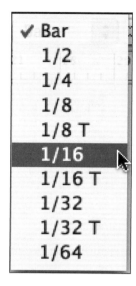

Figure 4.3

Setting the Snap value to 1/16.

Previewing Notes

Reason's Edit mode gives you the ability to preview notes, slices, or drum sounds for the selected instrument so you can find the tone you are looking for. For sampler and synth devices, you click the vertical keyboard display along the left side of the Key lane to preview the sound of that note. When you roll your mouse over the vertical keyboard along the left side, the cursor turns into a speaker icon with a plus sign underneath it (see Figure 4.4); click a note to preview that particular pitch on the selected device.

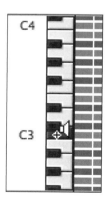

Figure 4.4

Previewing the note C3 in the Key lane of a SubTractor track.

You can also preview the 10 sounds of a Redrum device by clicking the appropriate channel along the left side of the Redrum's Drum lane. In Figure 4.5, there is a Redrum loaded up with Electronic

Kit 1. The 10 sounds are labeled stretching vertically along the left side. Clicking your mouse on each one of these cells enables you to preview each of the different drum sounds. Any adjustments you have made to the pitch, level, panning, and so on for these 10 channels will be heard when you click here to preview.

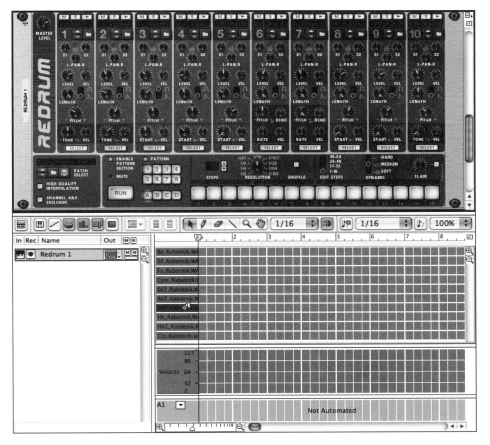

Figure 4.5

Previewing the BD3Rabotnik.wav sound in the Drum lane of the Redrum track.

The same technique applies when working with a Dr REX player. In Chapter 5, "Sequencing Beats in Reason," you will look at the various ways to sequence the Dr REX. One of these techniques involves drawing the notes directly into the REX lane. When you load up a Dr REX into Reason, you can preview the slices by clicking the slice number along the left side of the REX lane. The Dr REX device can handle REX loops with up to 92 total slices. As with the Key and Drum lanes, when you roll your mouse over the list of slices along the left side of the REX lane, it turns into a speaker icon with a plus sign, which enables you to preview the slices. Figure 4.6 shows Slice #3 being previewed.

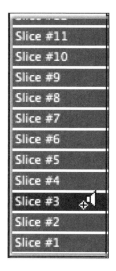

Figure 4.6

Previewing Slice #3 in the REX lane of the sequencer track for the Dr REX player.

Drawing In Notes

Drawing in notes is a great way to handle a complicated part that perhaps could take too long to perform perfectly. You can go right into the lane and draw in the notes exactly as you want your melody to sound. It can be a real time saver when programming drumbeats or bass lines. In the end, it really depends on how you like to work. Some people prefer to perform every part of their song, while others prefer to program their beats and melodies. Reason's Pencil tool and related quantization tools offer you the precision and flexibility you need to handle almost any compositional task.

To draw in notes, you merely need to have the Pencil tool selected in the toolbar, have the appropriate lane showing in the Edit mode, and then begin drawing in notes where you would like them. The Timeline (see Figure 4.7) along the top of the sequencer plays a key role in the process of drawing in notes because it acts as your guiding compass, showing you where you are in your song.

Figure 4.7

The Timeline stretches across the top of the sequencer.

When you are drawing in notes, you may find that you need to adjust the size of the viewable area. For example, when I am working on a small section of a song, I often find it necessary to zoom in closely to see exactly what is going on in the minutest moments of the piece. I do a lot of micro-editing with my compositions, especially when it comes to the drums; if I am not zoomed in close enough, I may not be able to see the grid with enough precision to properly place the appropriate drum hits where they need to be. You can either use the Magnify tool (it's the one with a magnifying glass on it, shown in Figure 4.8) in the toolbar for zooming purposes or you can use the Horizontal Zoom slider (see Figure 4.9), located in the lower-left corner of the sequencer.

Figure 4.8

The Magnify tool.

Figure 4.9

The Horizontal Zoom slider.

To draw in a note, just click the note display part of the lane at the desired position with the Pencil tool. To draw longer notes that are a multiple length of the Snap value, click the grid, hold down your mouse button, and drag to the right. Drawn notes will be constrained to the grid as defined by the Snap value if the Snap to Grid function is turned on. For example, if the Snap value is set to bar, then any notes drawn in will be a minimum length of one bar and longer notes will be constrained to be multiples of one bar. Thus, notes can be drawn of length one bar, two bars, three bars, and so on. If you want to draw in notes with greater detail, just decrease the Snap value and you can draw in notes of smaller lengths. If you wish to create a note length unconstrained by the grid's Snap value, hold down the Shift key while you drag to the right.

Note

If you make a mistake when drawing in a note, the quick and easy way to fix it is to simply undo the action. To do so, either choose Undo from the Edit menu or press Command·Z (Mac) or Ctrl·Z (Windows).

Here is an exercise to get you acquainted with drawing in notes:

1. Open the file DrawingNotes.rns on the included CD-ROM.
2. Click the Bass track in the sequencer. This is a SubTractor loaded up with a Bass Guitar patch.
3. Click the Switch to Edit Mode button. This allows you to see the Key lane.
4. Set the horizontal zoom so that you can see only the first two bars in the sequencer window.
5. Click the Pencil tool.
6. Set the Snap value to 1/16, and make sure the Snap to Grid function is turned on by clicking the Snap to Grid button (the one with a magnet on it).
7. Draw in a 1/16th note for the key C2 on the first beat of bar 1.
8. Draw in 1/16th notes for C2 on the second, third, and fourth beats of bar 1. Your screen should now look like the one shown in Figure 4.10.

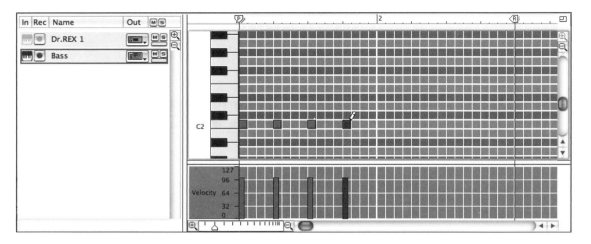

Figure 4.10

A C2 1/16th note drawn on each beat of the first bar in the Key lane of the Bass track in the sequencer.

9. Try drawing in a longer note. Click G2 right at the beginning of bar 2 and, with the mouse button pressed down, drag to the right to draw a note 3/16th long. This will fill three boxes on the 1/16th note grid. Your sequencer should now look like the one shown in Figure 4.11.

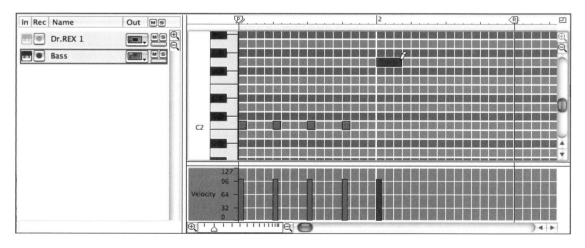

Figure 4.11

Drawing in a 3/16th length note G2 starting at bar 2.

Selecting Notes

After you have played or written notes into the sequencer, you may find that you need to move them around, delete them, or adjust their position or note length so they better fit in with the rest of your composition. You select notes in the sequencer by using the Selection tool (see Figure 4.12).

Figure 4.12
The Selection tool.

To select a note with the Selection tool, simply click the note. If you want to select multiple notes, hold down the Shift key and click each note you want to select. You can also click in the sequencer and drag to draw a rectangle around several notes, selecting them all at once (see Figure 4.13).

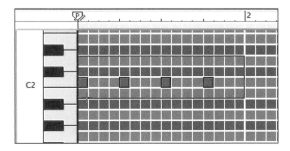

Figure 4.13
Select multiple notes by drawing a rectangle around them.

When you have selected a particular note, you can use the right and left arrow keys on your keyboard to select the next or previous note on the track. This is handy if you have a series of notes clustered together and you are trying to get at the one particular note that needs a slight adjustment. But what if the notes with the exact same position on the Timeline? Clicking the right arrow will progress through notes with the same starting point beginning with the note that has the highest pitch, moving down through these notes and then to the right.

You can select all the notes in a song by clicking somewhere in the appropriate lane (Key, Drum, REX, and so on), opening the Edit menu, and choosing Select All. Alternatively, you can use the Command+A (Mac) or Ctrl+A (PC) keyboard shortcut. To deselect all the notes after you have selected them, simply click anywhere in the background of that particular lane without clicking a note.

Note

If you already have the Pencil tool selected, you can switch to the Pencil tool by holding down the Command (Mac) or Ctrl (PC) key. This is a great trick for streamlining your workflow while drawing in notes and editing them. For example, say you draw in a note in the wrong place. You can easily flip over to the Selection tool, move the note, and return to the Pencil tool, ready to draw in more notes. Not having to keep clicking the toolbar to switch back and forth is a helpful timesaver.

Moving Notes

After you have played or written notes into the sequencer, you may find that you need to move them around, adjusting their position so they better fit in with the rest of your composition. You can easily move notes around in the sequencer using the Selection tool. To do so, click the desired note in the sequencer, hold down the mouse button, and drag the note to the desired location. With the Snap to Grid function turned on, moved notes retain relative distance to the grid defined by the Snap value.

Try doing a little exercise to practice moving notes:

1. Open the song MovingNotes.rns on the included CD-ROM.

2. Click the Bass track in the sequencer.

3. Click the Switch to Edit Mode button so you can see the Key lane.

4. Notice that in the melody in the Key lane, the C2 note that occurs just before bar 5 comes in a little early. To adjust is so that it comes in right on the first beat of bar 5, first, click the Magnify tool and zoom in for a closer view.

5. Activate the Snap to Grid function by clicking the Snap to Grid button (the one with a magnet) in the toolbar.

6. Click the Selection tool.

7. Click the early C2 note and move it so it comes in right at bar 5.

8. The Bass track's Key lane should now look like the one in Figure 4.14.

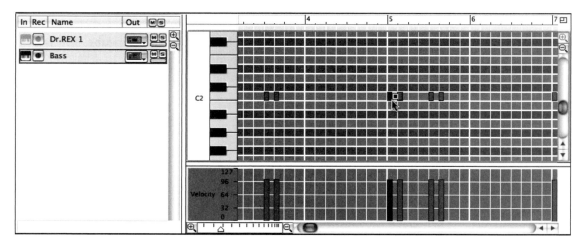

Figure 4.14

The C2 note is moved to hit right at the start of bar 5.

Copying Notes

If you hold down the Option (Mac) or Alt (PC) key while moving notes, the notes will appear with a green plus sign as you drag them, indicating that you are copying these notes (see Figure 4.15). This might come in handy if, for example, you have created a nice melody and you would like to repeat it; you can save time by highlighting all the notes and then copying them using this technique.

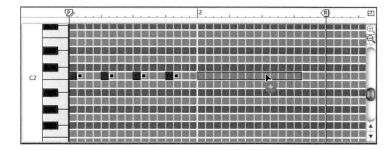

Figure 4.15

If you hold down the Option (Mac) or Alt (PC) key and dragging notes, a green plus sign appears, indicating that you are copying the notes.

You can also copy notes using the Copy command in the Edit menu. Highlight the notes you wish to copy, and open the Edit menu and select Copy; alternatively, use the Command+C (Mac) or Ctrl+C (PC) keyboard shortcut. When you copy notes, the position marker P automatically moves to the end of the selection; paste the copied notes by placing position marker P at the location where you want to paste the data.

Try doing a quick exercise to practice copying notes;

1. Open the file CopyingNotes.rns on the CD-ROM. Notice the four-bar melody in the Key lane of the Piano track

2. Click the Selection tool.

3. Set the Snap value to 1 bar.

4. Draw a rectangle around the first four bars of notes.

5. Open the Edit menu and choose Copy. Alternatively, use the Command+C (Mac) or Ctrl+C (PC) keyboard shortcut. Notice that after the notes have been copied, the position marker P moves to 5.1.1.

6. Paste these notes at bar 9 by grabbing the position marker P and moving it to position 9.1.1.

7. Open the Edit menu and choose Paste. Alternatively, use the Command+V (Mac) or Ctrl+V (PC) keyboard shortcut. Your sequencer should now look like the one in Figure 4.16.

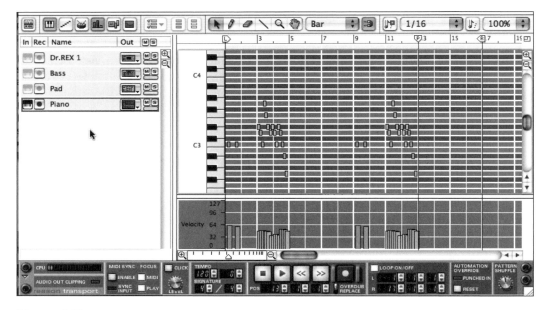

Figure 4.16

A sequencer with copied notes.

Resizing Notes

You can resize notes that you have drawn into the sequencer. When you select a note, a small square handle appears in the center of the note on right side. Click this handle and drag left or right to decrease or increase the length of the note. If the Snap to Grid function is on, the length of the note will be constrained by the Snap value.

Try completing a little exercise to practice resizing notes:

1. Open the file ResizingNotes.rns on the CD-ROM.

2. Click the Pad track in the sequencer.

3. Click Switch to Edit Mode so you can see the Key lane.

4. You see three bar-long notes. Let's change the first C3 note at bar 1 to be two bars long. To begin, click the Selection tool.

5. Click the C3 note at bar 1 to select it.

6. Activate the Snap to Grid feature by clicking the Snap to Grid button (the one with a magnet on it).

7. Click the square handle on the right side of the note and drag it out to make the note two bars long (see Figure 4.17).

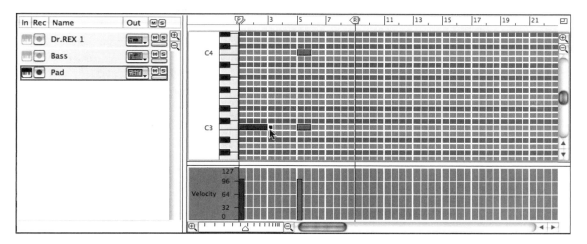

Figure 4.17

Resizing C3 to be two bars long.

8. Now, at bar 5, there are two bar-long notes: C3 and C4. Using the Selection tool, draw a box around both notes to select them (see Figure 4.18).

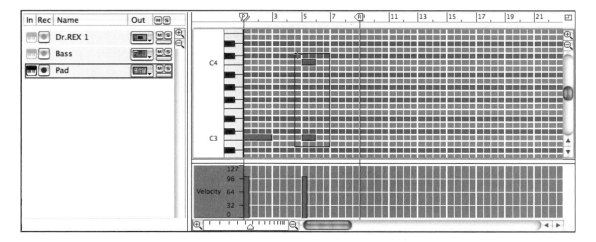

Figure 4.18

Draw a box around notes C3 and C4 at bar 5 to select them both.

9. Click the square handle on the right side of one of the notes and drag it out so that both notes become two bars long. Your Key lane should now look like the one in Figure 4.19.

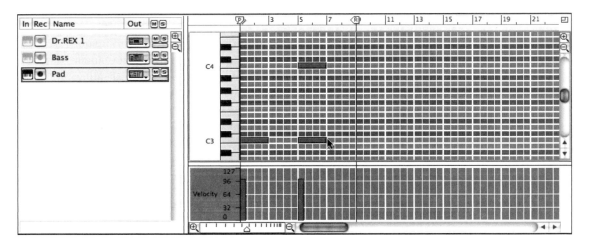

Figure 4.19
Resizing C3 and C4 at bar 5, making both be two bars long.

Deleting Notes

Deleting notes is as simple as clicking them with the Selector tool and then pressing the Backspace or Delete key on your keyboard. Alternatively, you can use the Eraser tool (see Figure 4.20). Simply click the Eraser button and then click individual notes to delete them. To delete a group of notes, click with the Eraser tool in the sequencer and draw a rectangle around the notes you want to delete.

Figure 4.20
The Eraser tool.

Try an exercise to practice deleting notes:

1. Open the file DeletingNotes.rns on the CD-ROM.

2. Click the Bass track in the sequencer.

3. Click Switch to Edit Mode so you can see the Key lane.

4. You see a couple of C2 1/16th notes and then a 1/2 note C#2 at bar 2. Let's delete this C#2 at bar 2. To begin, click the Selection tool.

5. Click the C#2 note at bar 2 to select it.

6. Open the Edit menu and select Delete. Alternatively, press the Delete or Backspace key.

7. Notice the four 1/16th notes between bars 6 and 7. Let's delete this cluster of notes using the Eraser tool. To begin, click the Eraser tool.

8. Click in the sequencer and draw a box around the four notes to delete them (see Figure 4.21). Your Key lane should look like the one in Figure 4.22.

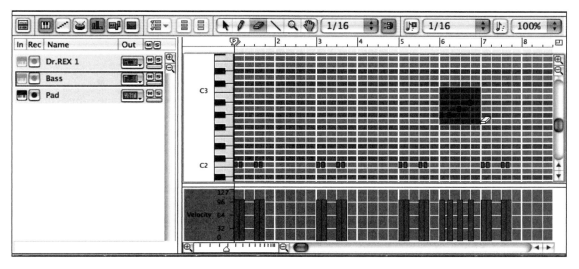

Figure 4.21
Draw a box around a group of notes with the Eraser tool to delete them.

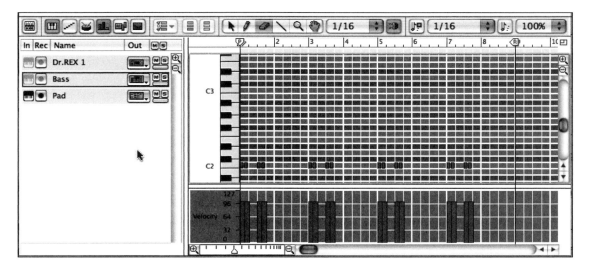

Figure 4.22
The Bass track's Key lane after the notes are deleted.

Importing/Exporting MIDI Files

Reason enables you to import standard MIDI files directly into the sequencer as well as export your work as a MIDI file. This allows you to easily transfer your work between Reason and other applications.

Exporting MIDI Files

You can export MIDI files out of Reason to be used in other applications or in some other context. Perhaps you have written a great melody, and you wish to bring that into another application to work with some of your other virtual instruments. Or maybe you are collaborating with friends who are also using Reason but you want them to select their own sounds for the various parts. Whatever the reason, it is easy to export MIDI. Here's how:

1. Open the file ExportMIDI.rns from the included CD-ROM. You'll see song with five different tracks in the sequencer.

2. Open the File menu and select Export MIDI (see Figure 4.23). This exports all the MIDI data in the sequencer to a standard MIDI file ending in .mid, keeping each lane of data intact.

Figure 4.23
Choose Export MIDI File from the File menu.

3. Give your new MIDI file a name and decide where to save it. For the sake of example, save this file to the desktop as glitchtechno.mid, because you are going to use it again in the next section.

Importing MIDI Files

There are a plethora of MIDI files on the web, and you can find MIDI files for most popular music by searching for MID files under the name of the song and artist you are looking for. Starting off with a MIDI file of a song is a great way to do a remix or a cover version. You can import it into Reason and then artfully select your sonic palette, assigning the different tracks of MIDI data to various instruments. To get the hang of importing MIDI files in Reason, try importing the MIDI file you just exported:

1. Open the file DefaultTemplate.rns on the included CD-ROM.

2. Open the File menu and select Import MIDI File (see Figure 4.24).

Figure 4.24

Choose Import MIDI File from the File menu.

3. Browse to your desktop and select the file glitchtechno.mid that you just exported. This loads five tracks of MIDI data into the sequencer (see Figure 4.25): Redrum Drums, Dr REX Drums, Sound FX, Bass, and Sub Bass.

83

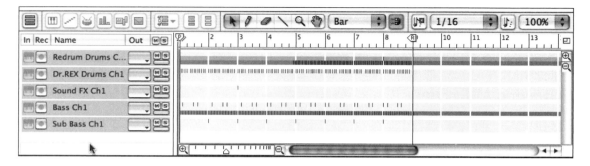

Figure 4.25

The sequencer loaded with an imported MIDI file.

4. Create a SubTractor by opening the Create menu and choosing SubTractor.

5. Load the SubTractor up with the Bass Guitar patch.

6. Assign the MIDI data in the Bass sequencer track to play the SubTractor. To do so, click the menu in the Bass track's Out column and select SubTractor (see Figure 4.26).

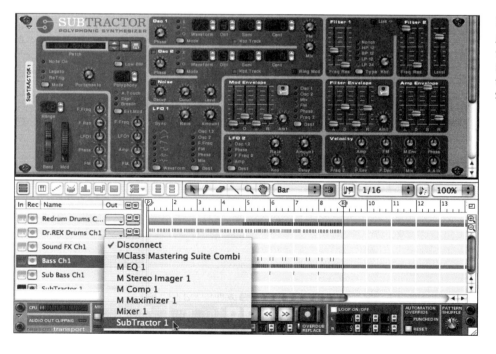

Figure 4.26

Assigning the MIDI data in the Bass track to the SubTractor.

5 Sequencing Beats in Reason

Many producers begin a new song by tracking the drums, or programming a beat, which then forms the backbone of the song. This chapter discusses how to sequence the Dr REX, using some of the REX files on the included CD-ROM. It also explores various ways of customizing your beats in order to differentiate yourself from others who use Reason, as well as experimenting with the addition of multiple Dr REX devices in order to mix things up.

In this chapter you will also look at the Redrum Drum Computer, a 10-channel step-programmable drum machine, each channel featuring its own set of controls for volume, pan, and so on. The Redrum can hold up to 32 patterns with as many as 64 steps each. In addition to looking at the various ways to sequence the Redrum, you'll see how you can create various patterns and then automate the pattern lane, or create a pattern and actually print the respective notes to the sequencer for further finessing. You can also use the Redrum as a sound module, playing the notes directly into the Drum lane.

In this chapter you'll learn to use the sequencer to get the most out of the Dr REX Loop Player. You will create several different Dr REX devices and load them up with clips. You will learn how to preview sounds, and then commit their patterns to the sequencer when you find a loop you like. After printing the data to the sequencer, you will do some tasteful manipulation of the resulting sequences and some selective editing of the various sections as well as become acquainted with Reason's Quantization function (discussed more thoroughly in Chapter 8, "Quantization"). When all is said and done, you will have a nice rhythmic foundation on which you will continue to build as the book proceeds.

Sequencing Dr REX

The Dr REX Loop Player is a device unique to Reason, capable of playing back and editing REX files at any tempo, maintaining the same pitch without losing sound quality. Reason's Factory Sound Bank comes complete with a nice collection of drum and percussion loops in a variety of musical styles to get you started (see Figure 5.1).

Figure 5.1

REX loops in the Reason Factory Sound Bank.

You can also use another application from Propellerheads, ReCycle, to create your own loops from sampled audio material. There are also a number of Reason ReFill libraries available from various content providers to further expand your library. Alternatively, you can pick up a CD that includes an assortment of individual REX files; they do not need to be in the form of a ReFill.

REX Files

REX files are initially created with ReCycle (see Figure 5.2), which is designed specifically for working with sampled audio loops. When loops are turned into REX files, they are essentially chopped into *slices*, with separate samples created for each individual beat. When playing back these REX files, the Dr REX Loop Player uses compression and stretching techniques that create a sort of liquid audio, retaining the pitch and punch of the original sample even at very different tempos.

For example, suppose you started with a loop of a bass line that had an original tempo of 120bpm and you were working on a song that is only 100bpm. Slowing the clip down turntable style would cause the pitch to change along with the tempo, and it would no longer match the rest of the song. Dr REX actually plays these REX files back in precisely the tempo of the song you are working on without any change in pitch or audible sound deterioration.

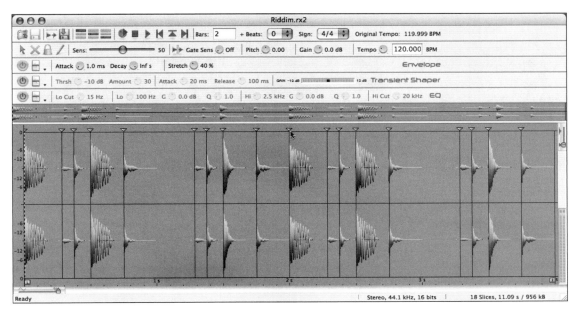

Figure 5.2

Create your own REX loops with Propellerheads' ReCycle.

Building a Foundation with Dr REX

Working with a Dr REX Loop Player is a good way to quickly build a solid foundation for your song. Most newcomers to Reason find the Dr REX device to be immediately gratifying, because you can use it to quickly whip up a professional-sounding beat. The key to differentiating yourself from all the other producers who are using Reason is to come up with creative ways of customizing these beats. This might involve using several different Dr REX devices together, alternating between loops, adding effects, and so on. Take a moment to practice using the Dr REX by completing the following exercise, which runs you through the basic steps for creating a Dr REX Loop Player, selecting a loop, and printing it to the sequencer.

1. Start by opening the file DefaultTemplate.rns on the included CD-ROM.

2. Click the Mixer 14:2 and add a Dr REX by selecting it from the Create menu. Reason automatically routes the Dr REX into the next open channel on the mixer.

3. Click the Browse Loop button on the left side of the Dr REX (it's the one with a folder on it, as shown in Figure 5.3) and browse to the location on your hard drive where you have copied the REX files content from the included Skill Pack CD-ROM.

4. You should see a number of REX loops in this folder; double-click the Riddim loop to load it into the Dr REX player.

Figure 5.3
Click the Browse Loop button on the blank Dr REX to load a REX file.

> **Note**
>
> In general, you do not want to run your sessions off of a CD-ROM. You will want to copy any ReFill libraries, WAV files for the samplers, or additional REX files you may have acquired to a folder on your hard drive for optimum performance.

5. You can pre-hear different loops in the Dr REX by clicking the Preview button on the device itself (see Figure 5.4), but in order to make your REX loop part of your song you must click the To Track button (see Figure 5.5) and print the MIDI data to the sequencer to create sequencer notes from the slices.

> **Note**
>
> A mistake commonly made by new Reason users is that they listen to their song with the Dr REX's Preview button turned on. Then, when they go to export their finished song as an audio file, it does not include this REX beat. Why does this happen? It is because the REX file was never properly printed to the sequencer. Although it is true that you can hear the REX loop playing along in time with the other material while it is being previewed, it is necessary to commit the data to the sequencer in order to actually add it to your song before you export it.

Figure 5.4

The Preview button lets you preview your REX loop in time with the global tempo.

Figure 5.5

Click the To Track button to send MIDI data to the sequencer track.

6. Suppose you want this loop to play for 16 bars; you will need to set the left and right locators to 1.1.1 and 17.1.1 respectively. To do so, grab the L and R markers on the Timeline above the sequencer and move them to the correct position (see Figure 5.6). Alternatively, adjust the L and R locator values in the Transport by clicking the up and down arrows to adjust the values for bar, beat, and 1/16th note, or by double-clicking the value and typing a new one. For example, typing **1.1.1** for the L marker moves it to the first bar, first beat, and first 1/16th note.

7. With the Dr REX device selected in the sequencer and the appropriate length determined by the L and R locator points, click To Track on the Dr REX interface. Reason will create a different note for each slice of the REX file, positioned in the sequencer according to the timing and length of the slices. The first note will be printed on C1, continuing upward in semi-tone steps, with one note per slice.

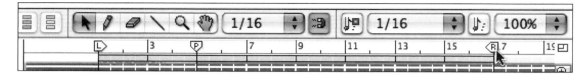

Figure 5.6
Setting the L and R locator points.

With the sequencer in Arrange mode, you see several identical groups of data in the Dr REX track. Each of these groups is the original length of the REX file. Because the Riddim loop with which you are working is a REX file that is two bars in length, and because you printed 16 bars to the sequencer, you should now see eight identical boxes of data (see Figure 5.7).

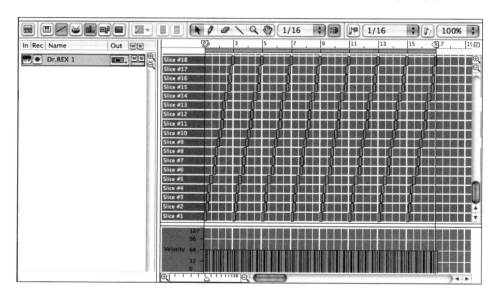

Figure 5.7
REX data printed in the sequencer (Arrange mode).

Adding a Second Dr REX

One technique that can help to differentiate your work from that of other producers using Reason is to layer or alternate between different REX loops. Using multiple Dr REX devices loaded with different loops can give your song some variety, help build energy, and keep the rhythm track moving along.

Let's now run through an exercise to create several Dr REX devices.

1. Create Dr REX Loop Player by selecting it from the Create menu.

2. Click the Browse Loop button.

3. Browse to the folder where you copied the content on the CD-ROM and select the Riddim.rx2 file.

4. Click the Preview button to hear what this patch sounds like at the song's tempo.

5. To create a 16-bar loop, set the L locator to 1.1.1 and the R locator to 17.1.1.

6. Click the To Track button on the Dr REX to create sequencer notes for each slice.

7. Create a second Dr REX Loop Player by selecting it from the Create menu.

8. Click the Browse Loop button.

9. Browse to the folder where you copied the content on the CD-ROM and select the HiHats.rx2 file.

10. Click the Preview button to hear what this patch sounds like at the song's tempo.

11. To create a 16-bar loop, set the L locator to 1.1.1 and the R locator to 17.1.1.

12. Click the To Track button on the Dr REX to create sequencer notes for each slice.

Now the sequencer has two tracks, each with a different Dr REX player and 16 bars of data. In the Arrange mode, this data appears as eight groups of data for the Dr REX 1 track and four groups of data for the Dr REX 2 track (see Figure 5.8).

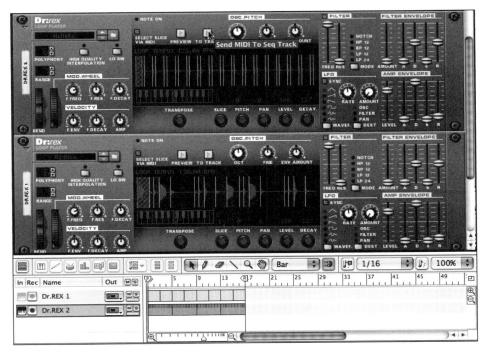

Figure 5.8
REX data for a second Dr REX printed in the sequencer (Arrange mode).

Renaming a Sequencer Track

When you start adding multiple Dr REX devices, it becomes more difficult to keep track of which one is the Riddim loop and which one is the HiHat loop. As you add devices to the sequencer, especially multiple instances of the same device, you may find it beneficial to rename the tracks to help you stay organized.

To rename a device, just double-click its name in the sequencer's track list to select it, and then type a new name. To practice, rename your two Dr REX Loop Players, changing the Dr REX 1 player to Riddim and the Dr REX 2 player to HiHat. This will help you keep better track of what file your Dr REX devices are loaded with (see Figure 5.9).

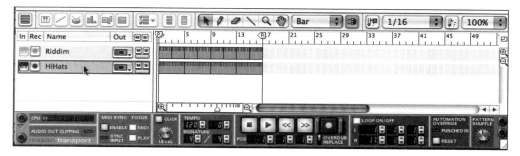

Figure 5.9
Renamed sequencer tracks.

> **Note**
>
> In addition to the method listed here, there are other ways to rename a device. You can rename a device by renaming the sequencer track, by double-clicking the little strip of tape on the corresponding channel on the mixer, or by clicking the name on the strip of tape along the left side of the device itself.

Alternating Beats by Deleting Groups of Data in Arrange Mode

Now that the REX data has been committed to the sequencer and your two tracks are renamed, it's time to return to your track and inject some variety into the beat by deleting every other group of data on the Riddim track. Leave the first two bars alone, but delete the second group of data that stretches from bar 3 to 5. To do so, click the Selection tool in the sequencer, click this group of data, and press the Delete or Backspace key on your keyboard. Alternatively, you can open the Edit menu and choose Delete. You can also use the Eraser tool. To create an alternating sequence, delete the groups between bars 7 and 9, bars 11 and 13, and bars 15 and 17. You can delete these groups one at a time or you can hold down the Shift key to select several groups and then delete them all at once. The sequencer should now look like the one in Figure 5.10.

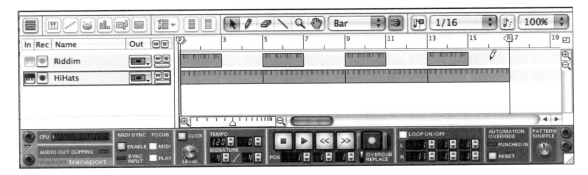

Figure 5.10

The sequencer in Arrange mode, after alternating groups on the Riddim track are deleted.

Adding a Third Dr REX

You now have two Dr REX players loaded with two different loops. When you click play, you hear these two loops together. It is a little bit loose, but they do in fact work together. Let's now add a third REX loop to the mix that has a drastically different feel.

1. Create a Dr REX by choosing it from the Create menu.

2. Click the Browse Loop button and browse to the folder where you copied the content from the CD.

3. Choose the Electro.rx2 REX loop.

4. Make sure the L and R locator points are set to 1.1.1 and 17.1.1.

5. Click the To Track button on this third Dr REX to print 16 bars in the sequencer. As shown in Figure 5.11, you now see four groups of data on this third track, each four bars long because the original REX loop was four bars long.

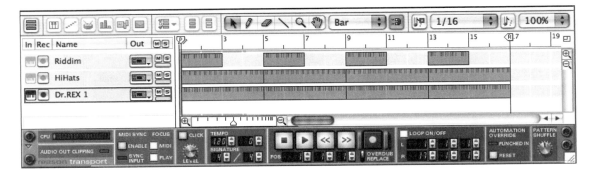

Figure 5.11

A sequencer with a third Dr REX player added and the data printed to track.

93

6. Click play; notice that this new Electro element severely clashes with what was already there. Fortunately, Reason has a great set of quantization tools, discussed next, that can help you fix this problem.

Quantization and Dr REX

Chapter 3, "Playing MIDI Notes," introduced the Quantize Notes During Recording function, which is used during MIDI recording to help tighten up a performed part. In addition to quantizing notes as they're added, you can also quantize material that is already in the sequencer, pushing the data closer to the a fixed value grid such as 1/4 note, 1/8th note, 1/16th note, one bar, and so on. Reason also has several included grooves that you can quantize to, as well as a special quantization feature, Get User Groove, which enables you to capture the feel of a groove from one rhythmic part or melody and then apply it to a different rhythm or melody. If you have several different loops with clashing rhythmic feels, the Get User Groove function allows you to capture the feel of one loop and then quantize another loop using the feel of this captured groove.

You'll dive deeper into Reason's quantization tools and at the Get User Groove function in Chapter 8, "Quantization." For now, you'll take a quick look at how you can use the quantization tools in the Reason sequencer to tighten up your REX loops and resolve this major groove incompatibility.

Because the Riddim track and the HiHats track sound okay together, let's concentrate on the Electro REX loop.

1. Click the Selection tool to activate it.

2. Click the sequencer just to the right of the end of the last group of data, hold down the mouse button, and drag to the left to draw a box around the four groups of data that comprise the Electro track (currently labeled Dr REX 1) to select them, as shown in Figure 5.12.

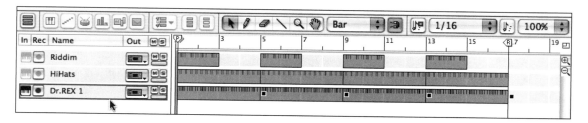

Figure 5.12
Groups of data highlighted on the Dr REX 1 track in the sequencer.

Note

You can quantize in either Arrange mode or Edit mode. Because you are interested in quantizing everything, use Arrange mode here. If you wanted only to quantize a select few notes or slices, you would select those notes in the Edit mode and quantize there. Again, you will thoroughly explore quantization in Chapter 8.

3. Establish the Quantization Value and the Strength of Quantization settings. For this example, choose 1/16 for Quantization Value and 100% for Strength of Quantization.

4. Between the Quantization Value and Strength of Quantization settings is the Quantize Notes button, which you click to actually execute the quantization on the selected notes. Click it now to shift all the REX slices that comprise these groups of data to land exactly on the 16th note grid.

5. Click play; notice that you can hear a big difference. The Dr REX 1 track no longer clashes so much. The Riddim track, however, is still a bit loose.

6. Select the four groups in the Riddim track by drawing a box around them, as shown in Figure 5.13.

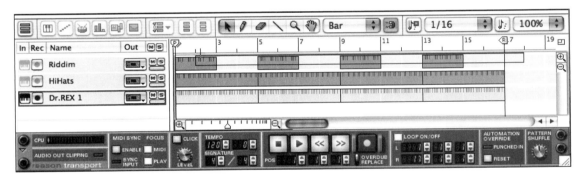

Figure 5.13

Draw a box around data in Riddim track

7. Click the Quantize button to quantize the REX slices that comprise these groups on the Riddim track.

8. Click play and listen to all three REX loops together. Notice that it sounds much tighter and does not clash as it did before.

Editing in the REX Lane

REX loops are composed of a number of slices of audio, corresponding to the elements that make up a particular drum beat. Slice #1 might be a kick drum, Slice #2 a hi-hat, Slice #3 a snare drum, Slice #4 another hi-hat, and so on. When you print the data from a Dr REX to the sequencer, it prints all the slices in the REX lane at the proper length and timing so that it maintains the original beat. That said, you do not have to stick to this recipe and maintain the original beat. In fact, you have a number of options at your disposal for creating your own beats from this material. You already looked at how you can use the Quantize function to change up the feel of a REX loop; now you will look at how you can actually edit and program beats directly into the REX lane.

In the ongoing example, you have three different Dr REX players loaded with three different loops. You quantized the Riddim and Electro beats to a 1/16th note grid and deleted every other two bars of the Riddim beat, creating an alternating pattern. Listening to what you now have, however, you'll find that there are still a few places where it gets a little sloppy even though you applied quantization. Listening more closely, you'll notice that there is some conflict in the kick-drum department, with the Riddim loop's kick drums doubling up and adding a bit of overkill with what is already going on in the Electro loop. You can take care of this problem by first identifying the slices in the Riddim loop that are these kick-drum hits and then deleting them in the REX lane.

1. Open the file EditingRexLane.rns on the CD-ROM. You will see three Dr REX devices along with three sequencer lanes named Riddim, HiHats, and Dr REX 1.

2. Rename Dr REX 1 to Electro so you can keep track of your work.

3. Click the Riddim track in the sequencer.

4. Click the Switch to Edit Mode button in the upper-left corner of the sequencer (see Figure 5.14). You should see the blue REX lane and red Velocity lane for the Riddim track (see Figure 5.15).

5. The name of each slice that makes up the REX loop is listed along the left side of the REX lane. To find the offending drum, preview each slice by hovering your mouse over the name of the slice and clicking the speaker icon that appears (see Figure 5.16). Moving up the list, you'll find that Slice #1 and Slice #10 are the kick sounds. Playing the song back, you can verify that these are in fact the places where a clash is happening and the doubled kick drum is unnecessary. Now that you've identified the culprits, let's get rid of them.

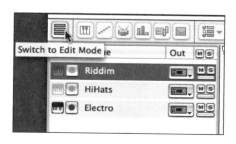

Figure 5.14

Highlight the Riddim track and click the Switch to Edit Mode button.

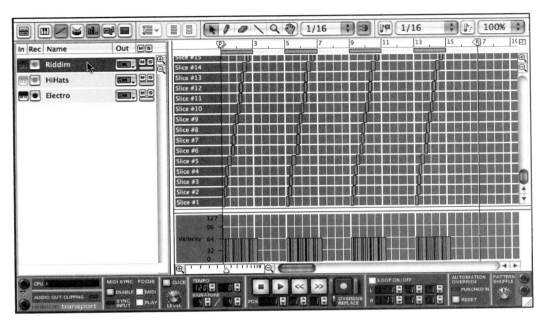

Figure 5.15

Edit mode reveals REX lane of the Riddim track for editing slices.

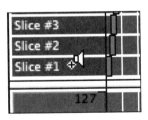

Figure 5.16

Roll your mouse over the slice name to preview an individual REX slice.

6. There are two ways to delete a slice from the sequencer. One is to use the Selection tool to click the slice (hold down the Shift key to select multiple slices) and then click the Delete or Backspace key. Alternatively, use the Eraser tool, located along the top of the Reason sequencer, to click the slice in the sequencer that you wish to erase. After deleting Slices #1 and #10 from the first group of data, your REX lane should look like the one in Figure 5.17.

7. You deleted these slices for the first group of data in the Riddim REX lane, but there are still three other groups of REX data on the Riddim track where the slices have *not* been deleted. You could go through and continue deleting each and every slice throughout the rest of the song, but because it is the same data as the first group, it makes more sense to just copy the first, already-edited group and paste it in those other places. To do this, switch back to Arrange mode by clicking the Switch to Arrange Mode button in the upper-left corner of the sequencer (see Figure 5.18).

97

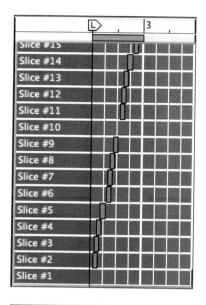

Figure 5.17

The Riddim REX lane after
Slice #1 and Slice #10 are deleted.

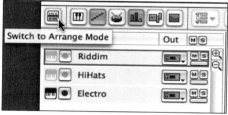

Figure 5.18

The Switch to Arrange Mode button.

8. In Arrange mode, you can see that there are four groups of data in the Riddim track in the sequencer. You have made changes to the first group of two bars; this is the group that you want to duplicate. First, however, delete the other three groups by drawing a rectangle around them with the Eraser tool (see Figure 5.19).

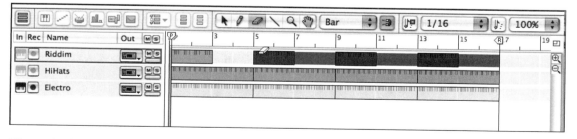

Figure 5.19

Draw a box around the other groups of data with the Eraser tool.

9. After deleting these three groups you are left with the edited group in red. To duplicate this group, click the Selection tool and, while holding down the Option (Mac) or Ctrl (Windows) key, click and drag the group to the right to begin at bar 5.

10. Copy the group again to begin at bar 9, and again at bar 13.

11. Switch back to Edit mode; your screen should now look like the one in Figure 5.20.

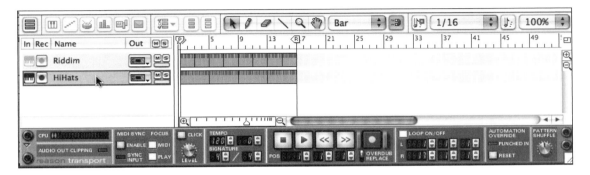

Figure 5.20
The Riddim track in Edit mode with the first group duplicated three times.

Programming the REX Lane

If you have a REX file that features particular slices that you really like—for example, perhaps the snare and the kick drum work for you but you don't like the rhythm—you can use the Pencil tool to draw in your own beat right into the REX lane, programming it as you see fit and leaving out the sounds that don't work for you. If you have a MIDI keyboard connected, you can also play in the rhythm. Let's take a look at how you can program a beat using the slices that comprise the Electro loop.

1. Click the Electro track in the sequencer and view the REX lane in Edit mode. (A shortcut to get there from Arrange mode is to just double click one of the groups of data in the Electro lane. This automatically switches over to the Edit mode and lets you work with the slices that comprise that group.)

2. Start building a one-bar loop for the next part of the song starting at position 17.1.1 and going until 18.1.1 by setting the left and right locator points correctly.

3. Now that you have the song set to loop for one bar, preview the slices by clicking them to find a sound you like. (Notice that if you hold down the mouse button, Reason will play the full length of the slice.)

4. Slice #2 is a nice kick-drum sound, so switch to the Pencil tool and get ready to draw it in beginning at bar 17.

99

5. The current Snap value is 1/16 and the Snap to Grid function is turned on. To change the Snap Value setting to 1/4 note for drawing in the kick drum, click the Snap Value menu and choose 1/4 (see Figure 5.21).

Figure 5.21

Changing the Snap Value setting from 1/16 to 1/4.

6. With the Pencil tool, click the note display part of the REX lane at the desired position, which is on the first beat of bar 17 for Slice #2. A 1/4 note will be drawn in at the closest Snap Value position.

7. Draw a 1/4 note kick drum (Slice #2) on beat 3 of bar 17.

8. Now that you have a kick on the 1 and 3, add a snare on beats 2 and 4.

9. Preview the slices along the left side of the REX lane; you'll discover that Slice #5 is a nice snare hit.

10. Draw in 1/4 notes on beats 2 and 4 of bar 17 so that the REX lane looks like the one in Figure 5.22.

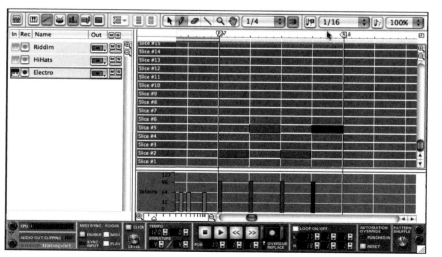

Figure 5.22

Draw in a 1/4 note kick drum (Slice#2) on beats 1 and 3 and 1/4 note snares (Slice #5) on beats 2 and 4 of bar 17.

11. You might decide after listening that you would like to have a double kick drum at bar 3—say, two 1/8th-note kick-drum hits instead of only one. To do this, first change the Snap Value setting to 1/8 (see Figure 5.23).

Figure 5.23

Changing the Snap Value setting from 1/4 to 1/8.

12. Using the Pencil tool, draw in 1/8th notes. You can add a second hit for the kick drum on the "and" of beat 3 such that if you were counting "one and two and three and four and," you would have kick-drum hits on both the "3" and the "and" following the third beat. Your REX lane should look like the one in Figure 5.24.

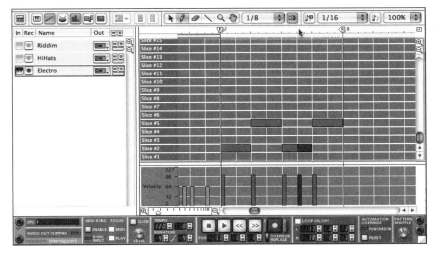

Figure 5.24

The REX lane with two successive 1/8th-note kick-drum hits on the third beat of bar 17.

13. Slice #3 is a nice hi-hat sound, so draw this in on all four "ands" of bar 17. If you have followed these steps and drawn in the notes correctly, your REX lane should look like the one in Figure 5.25.

Note

If you are counting out a beat as "one and two and three and four and" for a basic beat, kick drums usually happen on the one and three, snares on the two and four, and hi hats on the "ands".

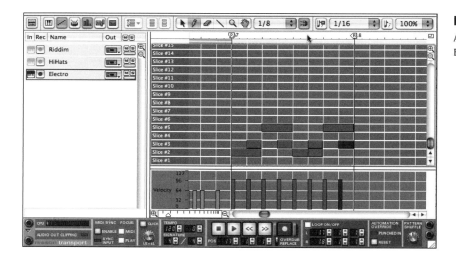

Figure 5.25

A basic beat on the Electro REX lane.

Sequencing Redrum

You just looked at Reason's Dr REX Loop Player, which enables you to quickly lay down a foundation on which to build. You explored some of the many ways to customize these REX beats and discovered methods by which to set your work apart from other producers using Reason. You may find, however, that you need more freedom than what the included REX loops provide. That is, after you get a certain amount of experience working with the program under your belt, you might discover that you want to program your own beats because doing so is a great way to make your productions unique. That's where the Redrum comes in. Reason's Redrum drum computer is fashioned after pattern-based drum machines such as the Roland 808 and 909, with 16 step buttons that are used for programming up to 32 different patterns.

There are two different ways to use the Redrum device. The first is to step program the Redrum. The second is to simply use it as a sound module and play the beats in with a MIDI controller. This section covers both methods of entering MIDI data into the sequencer. It also takes a look at the various tools that are available to edit data once it is in the sequencer.

The Redrum

The Redrum features 10 channels, each of which can be loaded with a separate audio sample. The Redrum supports WAV (.wav), AIFF (.aif), SoundFonts (.sf2), and REX file slices (.rex2, .rex, .rcy) of any bit depth or sample rate, stereo or mono. Regardless of their original bit depth or sample rate, the samples loaded into the Redrum will be stored internally in 16-bit format. There are individual controls over level, panning, sample length, and so on, which can be automated, as you will see later in this chapter.

You can load sounds for each of the 10 channels all at once by selecting one of the Redrum patches, which have the extension .drp. Reason comes with a number of different kits in various styles; these are located in the Reason Factory Sound Bank. These can be customized or you can create and save your own. To load an entire kit, click the Browse Patch button in the lower-left corner of the device (see Figure 5.26).

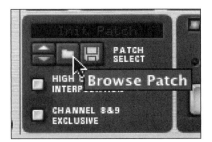

Figure 5.26
Loading a patch in the Redrum.

You can also choose to load individual samples by clicking the folder on each of the Redrum's 10 channels and then browsing and selecting an audio file (see Figure 5.27). The Reason Factory Sound Bank includes a nice selection of individual drum sounds, various one shots of kick, snare, hi-hat, percussion, Fx, and more. It is a great collection, and if you dig around a bit you'll find all kinds of interesting things.

Figure 5.27
Click the individual folder to load
sounds into individual Redrum channels.

Programming the Redrum

The Redrum features 16 step buttons that are used for programming up to 32 different patterns: A1–A8, B1–B8, C1–C8, and D1–D8. Up and down arrows enable you to set the total number of steps for each pattern (see Figure 5.28), which essentially is the length of the pattern before it starts repeating. Although each pattern can have up to 64 steps, the Redrum allows you to view only 16 steps at a time. An Edit Steps switch (see Figure 5.29) enables you to specify which steps you want to view and edit. It has four settings: 1–16, 17–32, 33–48 and 49–64. To keep it simple, let's start by programming a pattern with only 16 steps.

Figure 5.28

Up and down arrows for setting the total number of steps.

Figure 5.29

The Redrum's Edit Steps switch

1. Open the song RedrumStepProgram.rns on the CD-ROM.

2. Make sure that the Enable Pattern Selection and Pattern settings are activated on the Redrum (see Figure 5.30).

Figure 5.30

Activate the Enable Pattern Selection and Pattern settings on the Redrum.

3. Select the pattern you are going to create—in this example, choose A1.

4. To begin programming the beat, click the Select button on the bottom of the first channel (usually the kick drum, as it is here) to select it.

5. Click the various steps to program the beat. For a simple four-on-the-floor dance beat, activate steps 1, 5, 9, and 13 (see Figure 5.31).

Figure 5.31
A four-on-the-floor kick-drum pattern.

6. Program a snare-drum pattern on Channel 2. To begin, click the channel's Select button (see Figure 5.32).

Figure 5.32
Clicking the Select button enables step programming for that Redrum channel.

7. The Redrum offers three different values for programmed beats, which you adjust using the switch in the lower-left part of the Redrum: Hard, Medium, and Soft. For this example, switch it to the Hard setting (see Figure 5.33).

Figure 5.33
Use this switch to adjust the dynamic of your programmed Redrum beat.

8. Illuminate the step buttons 5 and 13 for a simple back-beat snare pattern on the two and four that is present in a lot of popular music (see Figure 5.34).

Figure 5.34
A basic snare pattern.

9. Continue with the remaining channels, programming a pattern for each of the sounds that you want to include in your rhythm.

Recording Pattern Automation

The yellow Pattern lane is where pattern changes can be automated for the Redrum as well as for Reason's other pattern-based device, the Matrix. After you have programmed several different patterns for the Redrum device, you can trigger these patterns and capture your performance. Reason records the pattern changes and plays them back just as you recorded them.

To record pattern changes, you must first record enable the sequencer track for the Redrum. Next, activate the Global Record button in the Transport. When you hit play, the sequencer captures any pattern changes that are made. You can use your mouse to click the numbers 1–8 and letters A–D to recall any of the 32 patterns.

Reason's Keyboard Control Function

If you find working with a mouse to be a bit limiting, you may want to try Reason's Keyboard Control function, which enables you to map the controls on any Reason device to keys on your typing keyboard. To use this feature, open the Options menu and choose Enable Keyboard Control. Next, open the Options menu and choose Keyboard Control Edit Mode. Everything in Reason now appears grayed out, with downward pointing yellow arrows on each of the controls on every device (see Figure 5.35). To map keys 1–8 on your typing keyboard to the pattern buttons 1–8 on the Redrum, double-click the yellow arrow on pattern button 1. The arrow turns into a spinning yellow box (see Figure 5.36); press the 1 key on your typing keyboard and a 1 appears on the Redrum, letting you know that pattern button 1 is now mapped to the 1 on your typing keyboard (see Figure 5.37). Continue this process for all eight of the pattern buttons, mapping button 2 to the number 2 on the typing keyboard, and so on. When finished, your screen should look like the one in Figure 5.38. Wrap things up by opening the Options menu and choosing Keyboard Control Edit Mode to uncheck it. Now, when you press the numbers 1–8 on your typing keyboard, it will change the pattern on the Redrum. I find this a much smoother way to change patterns than clicking the mouse—more like working with actual hardware.

Figure 5.35
Keyboard Control Edit mode.

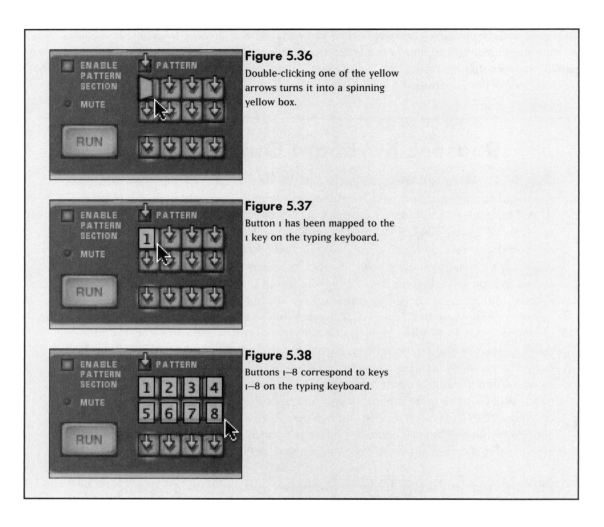

Figure 5.36

Double-clicking one of the yellow arrows turns it into a spinning yellow box.

Figure 5.37

Button 1 has been mapped to the 1 key on the typing keyboard.

Figure 5.38

Buttons 1–8 correspond to keys 1–8 on the typing keyboard.

Drawing In Pattern Automation

After you have programmed a few different patterns, you can use the Pencil tool in the sequencer's Pattern lane to automate the track. Try completing this exercise on drawing in pattern automation.

1. Open the file RedrumPatterns.rns on the CD-ROM. You will see a song loaded with an MClass Mastering Suite, a Mixer 14:2, a SubTractor loaded with a bass patch, and a Redrum with sounds on each of the 10 channels.

2. Click the Redrum track in the sequencer.

3. Click the Switch to Edit Mode button in the upper-left area of the sequencer. You should now see three lanes: the Drum lane, the Velocity lane, and the yellow Pattern lane.

4. Click the upside-down triangle on the left side of the Pattern lane to reveal a menu with a list of the 32 patterns, A1–A8 through D1–D8 (see Figure 5.39). Select pattern A3; This will be your main drum section.

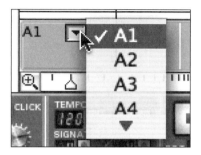

Figure 5.39
The Pattern Selection menu in the Pattern lane.

5. Click the Pencil tool.

6. Change the Snap Value setting from 1/16 to Bar.

7. Click anywhere on the Pattern track with the Pencil tool to draw pattern A3 across the entire length of the song (see Figure 5.40).

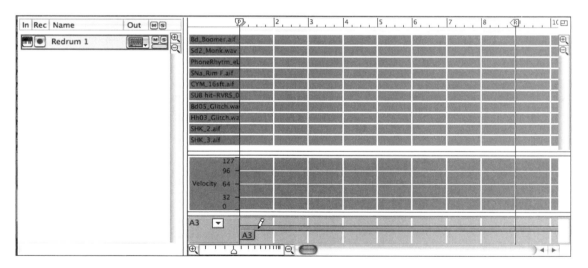

Figure 5.40
Pattern A3 selected for the entire song.

8. Select pattern A2 from the list.

9. Pattern A2 is a fill. Let pattern A3 go for six bars from bar 1 to bar 7, and A2 from bar 7 to bar 9.

10. With the Pencil tool, click the Pattern lane at 7.1.1. Hold down the mouse button and drag to the right from bar 7 to bar 9. You should now see pattern A3 from bar 1 to bar 7, pattern A2 from bar 7 to bar 9, and pattern A3 again from bar 9 until the end of the song (see Figure 5.41).

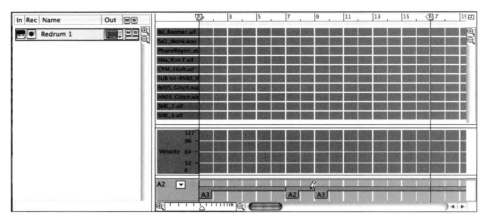

Figure 5.41

Pattern A2 from bar 3 to bar 5, and pattern A3 everywhere else.

11. Select pattern A1 from the list. This is a different fill pattern, which you will use from bar 15 to bar 17.

12. Using the Pencil tool, click bar 15 and drag to the right to bar 17 (see Figure 5.42).

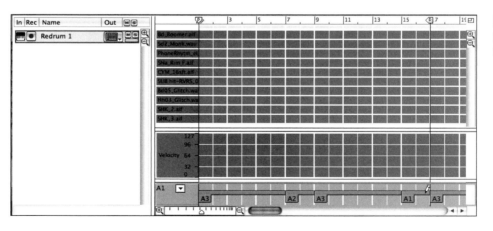

Figure 5.42

Pattern A1 from bar 7 to bar 9.

13. Open RedrumPatternsAfter.rns on the CD-ROM and check your work.

Copying Pattern Automation

You can edit the pattern-change information in the Pattern lane. For example, suppose you have drawn in a series of pattern changes on the first 16 bars and you want to duplicate that series several times. To do so, click the Selection tool in Edit mode, select bars 1–17 in the Pattern lane (see Figure 5.43), and open the Edit menu and choose Copy or press Command+C (Mac) or Ctrl+C (PC) to copy those 16 bars of pattern-change information to the clipboard. The position marker P automatically moves to bar 17, as shown in Figure 5.44; open the Edit menu and select Paste or press Command+V (Mac) or Ctrl+V (PC) to paste the selected bars. The results should look like the screen shown in Figure 5.45.

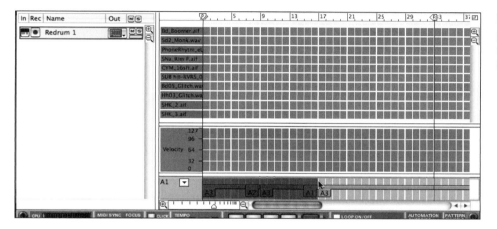

Figure 5.43

Highlight bars 1–17 in the Pattern lane.

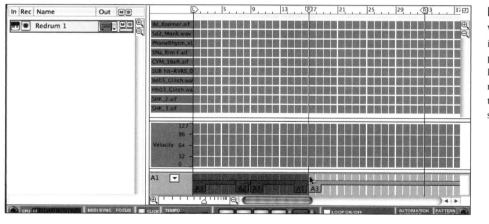

Figure 5.44

When copying information, position marker P automatically moves ahead to the end of the selected area.

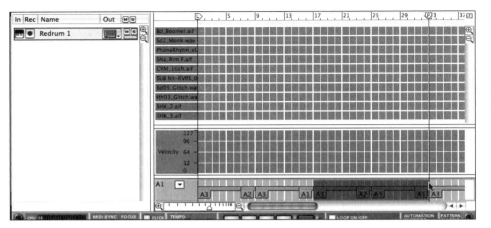

Figure 5.45

The Pattern lane after the first 16 bars have been copied and pasted.

Deleting Pattern Automation

To delete a section of pattern-change automation, simply select the bars you want to delete in the Pattern lane, open the Edit menu, and select Delete. Alternatively, select the bars you want to delete and press the Delete or Backspace key on your keyboard. You can use the Eraser tool as well. When you delete information in the Pattern lane, the pattern that was playing just before the time interval that you deleted will be extended all the way to the end of the time interval.

The Drum Lane

The Drum lane is broken into 10 vertical rows that correspond to each of the 10 drum channels on the Redrum itself. If a particular sequencer track is connected to a Redrum, you can use this lane to edit drum MIDI data. You can choose to print your programmed patterns into the Drum lane for further editing and manipulation or you can use the Redrum as a sound module and play in a beat with your MIDI controller.

Transferring Redrum Step Sequences to the Sequencer

After you have a pattern programmed on the Redrum, you can commit that data to the Drum lane in the Redrum's sequencer track using the Copy the Pattern to Track function. After the data printed in the Drum lane, you can go back over it and make fine adjustments, apply quantization to it, copy and paste it, and so on.

Say for this example that you want to print the pattern A1 to the sequencer. Here's how it's done:

1. Open the file RedrumPatterns.rns from the included CD-ROM.

2. Click the Redrum and select A1.

3. Use the left and right locator points to set the area in which you want to print this information to the sequencer. In this case, let's make an eight bar loop; set the L locator point to 1.1.1 and the R locator point to 9.1.1.

4. Open the Edit menu and choose Copy Pattern to Track, as shown in Figure 5.46.

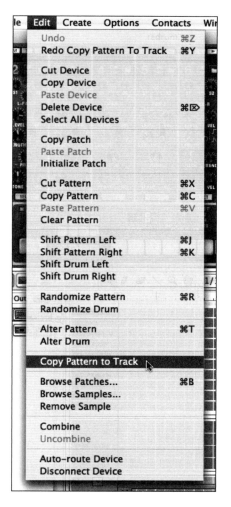

Figure 5.46
Select Copy Pattern to Track in the Edit menu.

5. Click the Redrum track in the sequencer (make sure you are in Edit mode). The Drum lane should be filled with all the corresponding MIDI notes that were programmed with the step-programmable buttons (see Figure 5.47).

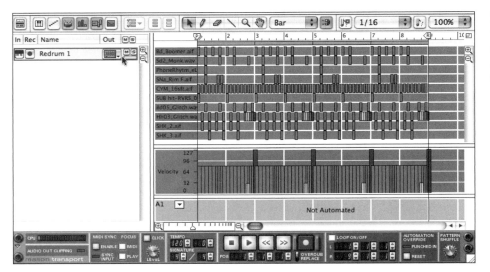

Figure 5.47

The Drum lane with the pattern copied to the track.

Using Redrum as a Sound Module

You can use the Redrum as a sound module or as a pattern-based device. That is, you can create several patterns and automate them in the sequencer's Pattern lane, or you can choose Copy the Pattern to Track to place the programmed notes into the sequencer's Drum lane in the area designated by the locator points. When you use the Redrum as a sound module, the 10 channels on the unit correspond to 10 consecutive keys on your MIDI keyboard. That is, channel 1 corresponds to the key C1, channel 2 to C#1, continuing up to channel 10, which corresponds to A1. Working in this manner, you can set up a loop and then play in your beat, focusing on several sounds at a time.

Drawing In Notes in the Drum Lane

You can use the Pencil tool to draw MIDI notes directly into the Drum lane. Thus, you can program your own beat this way if you prefer. To get the hang of drawing notes directly into the Drum lane, try this exercise:

> **Note**
>
> Different people have different approaches to working with Reason. Some prefer to program their beats on the Redrum using patterns while others prefer to play in the notes and still others would rather see a grid and draw in the notes that way. You thoroughly explored drawing in MIDI notes in Chapter 4, "Drawing In MIDI Notes."

1. Open the file DefaultTemplate.rns on the CD-ROM.

2. Create a Redrum by choosing the device from the Create menu.

3. Click the Browse Patch button.

4. Load the kit REDRUMDrawNotes, located on the CD-ROM.

5. Click the Switch to Edit Mode button.

6. Click the Pencil tool.

7. Grab the boundary between the sequencer and the rack and extend the sequencer upward so you can see all 10 channels of the Drum lane (see Figure 5.48).

Figure 5.48
Grab the boundary between the sequencer and the rack to expand the sequencer.

8. You're going to make a two-bar loop. To begin, move the L and R locator points to 1.1.1 and 3.1.1, respectively.

9. Using the Horizontal Zoom slider in the lower-left corner, enlarge the working area so that the first two bars fit completely in the screen.

10. Channel 1 features a bass drum, BD_Boomer. Draw in 1/16th-note kick-drum hits on the first and third beat of the first two bars (see Figure 5.49).

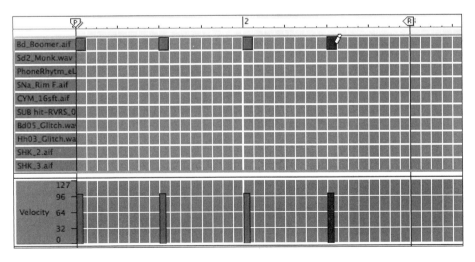

Figure 5.49
Drawing in a bass-drum pattern.

11. Draw in a snare pattern for the sound in channel 2 called Sd2_Monk. Add a snare hit on the second and fourth beat of the first bar, and then only on the fourth beat of the second bar (see Figure 5.50).

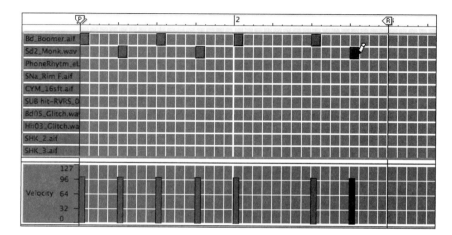

Figure 5.50

Drawing in snare-drum pattern.

12. Draw in a note on the fourth beat of bar 1 for the PhoneRhythm_eLab sound in channel 3.

13. Channel 4 features a rim shot called SNa_RimF. Draw in notes on the second and fourth beat of bar 1, and then on the fourth beat of bar 2.

14. Mixing it up, draw in notes on the fourth and sixth 1/16th notes of bar 2. The resulting pattern should look like the one in Figure 5.51.

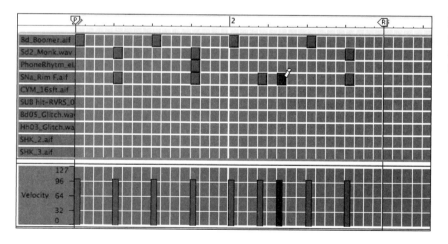

Figure 5.51

Drawing in a pattern for channels 3 and 4 of Redrum

15. Channel 5 has a hi-hat cymbal called CYM_16sft. Draw in a series of notes starting with the very first beat of bar 1, and then altering every other 16th note for two bars.

16. Between the last two notes you drew, add another note, but change the velocity on this note. To do so, click with the Pencil tool in the note's Velocity lane and draw it in at about half the velocity of all the other notes. It should appear a faded shade of pink compared to all the other red notes (see Figure 5.52).

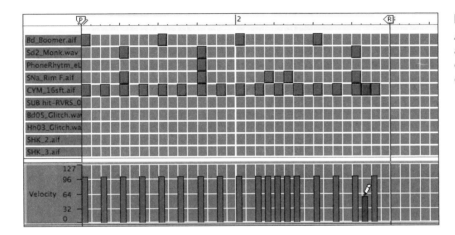

Figure 5.52

Adjusting the velocity for a note that is part of the cymbal pattern drawn on channel 5 of the Redrum.

17. Channel 6 features SUB hit-RVRS_01. Draw in a note on the very first beat of bar 1.

18. Channel 7 features Bd05_Glitch. You'll use this to fortify your snares, drawing it in on the second and fourth beat of bar 1 and then only on the fourth beat of bar 2 (see Figure 5.53).

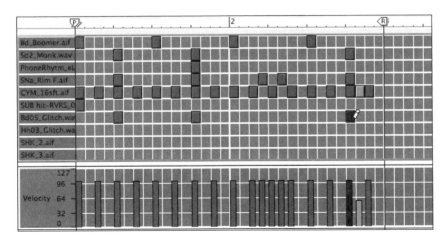

Figure 5.53

The pattern for channels 6 and 7.

19. Channel 8 has Hh03_Glitch. Draw this in on the "and" of both bars, but mix it up on the third beat of bar 2 by deleting the beat and drawing in a note on either side of where the beat was (see Figure 5.54).

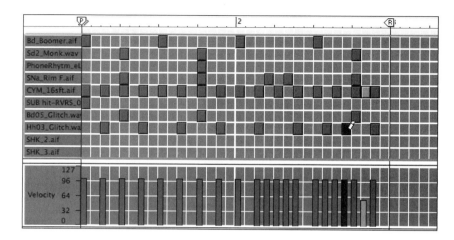

Figure 5.54
The pattern for channel 8.

20. Draw in a pattern for SHK_2 on every "and" of both bars.

21. Draw in a note on the first and third "and" of both bars for SHK_3. Your final pattern should look like the one in Figure 5.55; open RedrumDrawNotesAfter.rns and check your work.

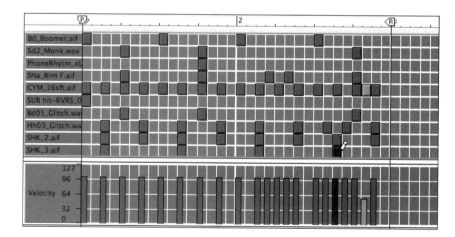

Figure 5.55
Final pattern for all 10 channels.

6 Editing MIDI Notes

So far, you have looked at the various ways to enter MIDI data into the Reason sequencer. In this chapter, you will take an in-depth look at the tools available for editing this data. Whether you have played or programmed the notes into the sequencer, Reason has a number of powerful features for editing your arrangement and making adjustments to your data. In this chapter, you'll go over some techniques for grouping various sections of your song together to create building blocks that will help you in the arrangement process. You will also take a look at some of the great features of the Change Events dialog box, which enable you to make broad changes to the pitch, velocity, and position of the data.

> **Note**
> Basically, this chapter introduces you to the sort of editing you will do in the course of producing a song. The best way to improve your skills is to practice, and the best way to practice is by creating new music. The beautiful things about Reason are its flexibility and power. Each time I sit down to work on a new piece, I discover some new way of working with the application. Reason is fantastic for experimentation, giving you the ability to wire up all these different devices in crazy ways that you just can't do in the hardware world without overrunning your studio with cables and gear. After you have mastered these basic editing functions, you will find it becomes quite easy to quickly develop your ideas into fully realized pieces.

Editing Tools

Unless you are a master keyboard player or a machine, chances are at some point you will have to make adjustments to some of the data you entered into the sequencer. Fortunately, Reason comes equipped with a variety of tools for making these types of adjustments to your MIDI note data.

In this section, you will learn about the two most-used tools for correcting mistakes: the Selection tool (see Figure 6.1) and the Eraser tool (see Figure 6.2). You use the Selection tool to select and move notes or group of notes, while the Eraser tool is used to erase individual notes, groups, or controller data. The quantization tools (see Figure 6.3) are also used fairly often for editing; they enable you to move recorded notes to (or closer to) an exact note-value position. You can use quantization to tighten up a performance, correct mistakes, or change the feel. You will explore the quantization tools in depth in Chapter 8, "Quantization."

Figure 6.1
The Selection tool.

Figure 6.2
The Eraser tool.

Figure 6.3
The quantization tools.

Adjusting Notes and Events

When recording a part by playing it in with a MIDI keyboard, a complete train wreck might be enough to force you to hit the stop button and start over again. But if you make only a minor timing error or hit a wrong note, odds are you will keep going if you are on a roll. You would most likely finish your performance and then go back to make any necessary adjustments. When drawing notes into the sequencer, however, you'll most likely immediately realize that you need to make an adjustment after entering a wrong note. Whether the data in the sequencer has been programmed or performed, the same techniques apply to making these adjustments.

Moving Notes

Moving notes is as easy as choosing the Selection tool, clicking the note in question in the sequencer, and then dragging the note to the desired location. When you move notes in the sequencer, their position is constrained by the Snap Value setting if the Snap to Grid function is turned on. If you want to move notes around the sequencer without having them constrained to the grid, just turn the Snap to Grid function off.

> **Note**
> I often work with a smaller Snap Value setting, such as 1/16, when I am drawing in notes and then switch to a larger value, such as Bar, when I need to move notes around. This smaller value allows me to have more detail when I am drawing in the notes, while the larger setting gives me the ability to retain the whole melody and the individual notes' relative positions on the grid when moving a selection of notes around.

To practice moving notes around, complete this exercise:

1. Open the file MoveNotes.rns on the CD-ROM.

2. Click the Switch to Edit Mode button.

3. Click the Keys sequencer track; you'll see a number of 1/16th notes and a few whole notes.

4. Suppose you want this melody to start four bars later so that you have four bars of drums before the melody kicks in. To begin, click the Selection tool.

5. Change the Snap Value setting from 1/16 to Bar (see Figure 6.4).

Figure 6.4

Changing the Snap Value setting from 1/16 to Bar.

6. Using the Selection tool, draw a box around the notes in the first four bars to select them.

7. Click one of the notes and drag it to the right to move the entire bunch so it begins at bar 5. The sequencer should now look like the one in Figure 6.5.

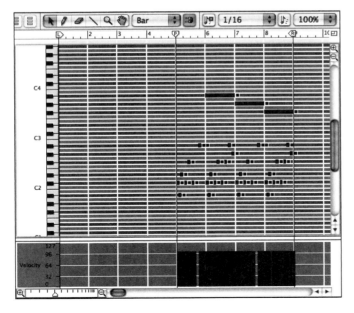

Figure 6.5

Moving the cluster of notes to begin at bar 5.

Duplicating Notes

If you hold down the Option (Mac) or Alt (PC) key while moving notes, the notes will appear with a green plus sign as you drag them, indicating that they are being copied (see Figure 6.6). If you have created a nice melody and you want to repeat it, you can save time by selecting all the notes and copying them using this technique.

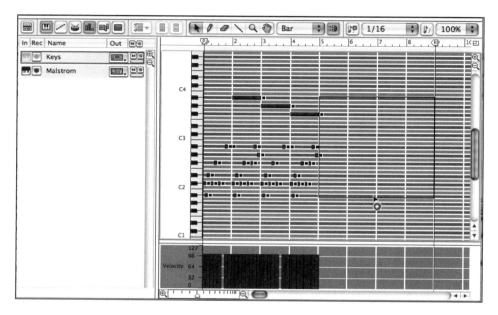

Figure 6.6

When notes are copied, a green plus sign appears.

Try completing this exercise to practice duplicating notes:

1. Open the file DuplicatingNotes.rns on the CD-ROM.

2. Click the Malström track.

3. Switch to Edit mode. In the Key lane, notice that there is now a melody from bar 1 to bar 5.

4. Click the Selection tool.

5. Draw a box around the notes from bar 1 to bar 5 to select them.

6. While holding down Option (Mac) or Alt (PC) key, click the selected notes, hold down the mouse button, and drag the notes to the right so that they begin at bar 9. A green circle with a plus sign appears to let you know that you are duplicating notes. Your sequencer should look like the one in Figure 6.7.

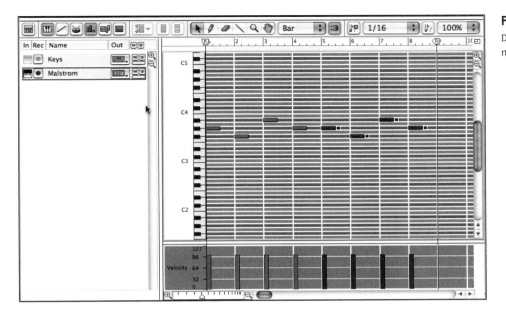

Figure 6.7

Duplicating notes.

Deleting Events

There are several ways to remove notes from the Reason sequencer. One is to use the Selection tool to select them and then open the Edit menu and choose Delete. Alternatively, you can delete selected notes by pressing the Delete or Backspace key on your keyboard. Finally, you can delete notes or events in the sequencer by using the Eraser tool. Simply click the Eraser tool and then click notes with it to delete them. If you have a group of notes you would like to erase, you can drag the Eraser tool to draw a box around them; all the notes in the box will be deleted.

To practice deleting events, try this exercise:

1. Open the file DeletingEvents.rns on the included CD-ROM.

2. Click the 'Keys' sequencer track.

3. Click the Switch to Edit Mode button. You should now see a bunch of notes in the Key lane.

4. Hit play and listen to this melody. Notice that a definite clash occurs at bar 4; the note D3 doesn't fit with the rest of the melody.

5. Click the Selection tool.

6. Click the note D3 at bar 4 to select it (see Figure 6.8).

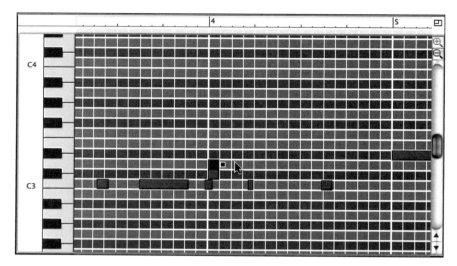

Figure 6.8

Select the offending C#4.

7. Open the Edit menu and choose Delete or simply press the Delete or Backspace key on your keyboard.

8. Listen further; you'll hear a clash at bar 8—another D3 that does not fit.

9. Click the Eraser tool.

10. Click the offending D3 on bar 8.

11. Listen further and notice that starting at bar 12 and ending at bar 13, there is a cluster of notes that does not fit with the rest of the melody—three B3 notes and an A3 note.

12. Use the Eraser tool to draw a box around the cluster of four notes that starts at B3 on bar 12 and goes to bar 13, leaving the melody in the lower octave alone (see Figure 6.9). Your sequencer should look like the one in Figure 6.10.

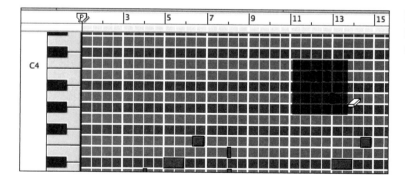

Figure 6.9

Delete a cluster of notes by drawing a box around it with the Eraser tool.

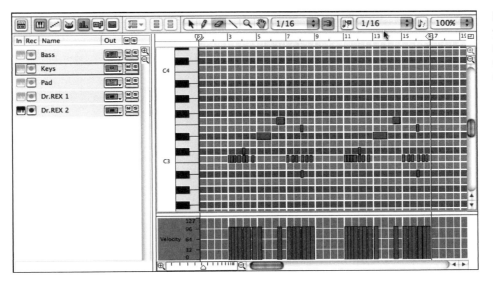

Figure 6.10
The sequencer after all the offending notes are deleted.

Adjusting Song Sections

When you are composing and arranging your music, often you will create parts that you will repeat in various places throughout the song. One melody might become the verse, another the chorus, and so on. Reason enables you to create a group of data, essentially bunching together a series of notes into one unit, that can then be used as a building block as you create your song's arrangement.

Creating a Group

You create groups in Arrange mode either by using the Pencil tool or by opening the Edit menu and choosing Group (see Figure 6.11) or pressing Command+G (Mac) or Ctrl+G (PC). First, however, you use the Selection tool to select the stretch of time in the sequencer that contains the events you with to group. Groups appear as colored boxes, with groups that contain the same data boxed in the same color. If you select data across several different tracks to be grouped, one group will be created for each track.

You can also use the Pencil tool to create a group. In the appropriate track in the sequencer, click the Pencil tool where you want the group to start, drag to the right, and release the mouse button where you want the group to end (see Figure 6.12). The length of a group will be constrained by the Snap Value setting if the Snap to Grid function is active, indicated by the illuminated magnet button in the toolbar.

Figure 6.11

Choose Group from the Edit menu.

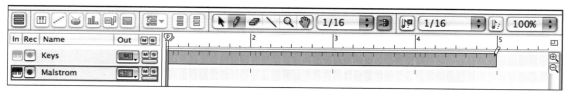

Figure 6.12

Creating a group with the Pencil tool.

Try this exercise, which covers both methods for creating groups:

1. Open the file CreatingGroup.rns on the CD-ROM. This file contains several tracks of data in the sequencer; you'll focus on the Malström track.

2. Click the Selection tool.

3. Click the Switch to Arrange Mode button.

4. Set the Snap Value setting to Bar.

5. Click and drag a rectangle around bars 1–5 in the Malström to select them.

6. Open the Edit menu and choose Group or press the Command+G (Mac) or Ctrl+G (PC) keyboard shortcut. Your sequencer should look like the one in Figure 6.13.

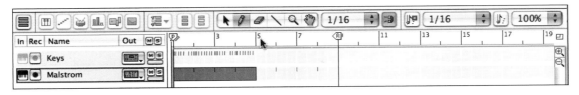

Figure 6.13

A group created from bar 1 to bar 5.

7. Next, use the Pencil tool group the data from bar 5 to bar 9. To begin, click the Pencil tool.

8. Make sure the Snap to Grid function is on and that the Snap Value is set to Bar. Then click at bar 5, hold down the mouse button, and drag to the right to bar 9. Your sequencer should look like the one in Figure 6.14.

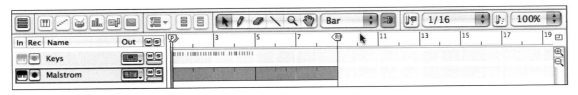

Figure 6.14

A second group, created from bar 5 to bar 9.

Selecting Groups

You can use the Selection tool to select groups of data in Arrange mode. Holding down the Shift key while clicking enables you to select multiple groups at once. You can also draw a box around several groups of data to select all of those groups at once (see Figure 6.15). After you have selected a group or several groups of data, you can move them around the sequencer, delete them, or perform an editing function on them.

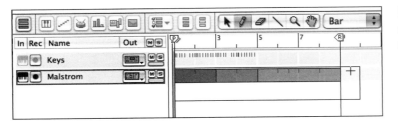

Figure 6.15

Draw a box around several groups to select them all at once.

Opening the Edit menu and choosing Select All or pressing Command+A (Mac) or Ctrl+A (PC) in Arrange mode selects all groups and events in the sequencer, across all lanes and tracks. Select All is handy if, say, you create a nice song but realize afterward that you want to add a 16-bar intro. Simply use the Select All function and move everything to the right by 16 bars. (Moving groups is discussed next.)

Moving Groups

You can move groups of data around in Arrange mode. For example, suppose you created a nice section of a song but then realized you want the section to come in at a different point in the song. If you group the melody together as one complete unit, you can easily move the group to a different location instead of trying to wrangle up individual notes and events. Groups can be moved to a different location on the same sequencer track or to a different track altogether.

If you hold down the Option (Mac) or Alt (PC) key while moving a group, a small plus sign appears letting you know that you are making a copy of the data. When you release the mouse button, a copy of the group is created at the new location. Using the Option/Alt shortcut key is very handy when you are arranging your track. It allows you to streamline your workflow. The more timesaving tricks like this you can learn, the easier you will find Reason to work with.

To practice moving around a group of data, do the following:

1. Open the file MovingGroup.rns on the included CD-ROM. Notice that there are several tracks of data in the sequencer; on the Dr REX Dub track, you see an eight-bar group of data highlighted in green.

2. Click the Selection tool on the toolbar.

3. Change the Snap Value setting to Bar.

4. Click the green group of data and drag it so it begins at bar 5. Your sequencer should now look like the one shown in Figure 6.16.

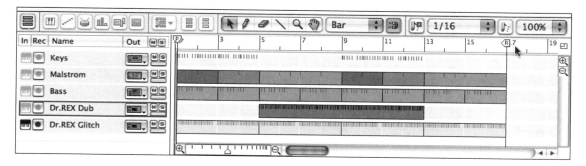

Figure 6.16

A group of data moved to begin at bar 5 on the Dr REX Dub track.

Deleting Groups

To delete a group of data, first select the group with the Selection tool and then open the Edit menu and choose Delete or simply press the Delete or Backspace key on your keyboard. Alternatively, select the Eraser tool and click the group you wish to delete. If you want to delete several groups at once, use the Eraser tool to draw a box around the groups.

I often find myself deleting groups when working with a Dr REX player. When you print the REX data to the sequencer track for a Dr REX, it fills in the entire length indicated by the left and right locator points. One of the things I like to do to give a song some variety is to alternate Dr REX beats. An easy way to do this is to delete every other group in the sequencer. To practice this, do the following:

1. Open the file DeletingGroup.rns on the included CD-ROM.

2. Open the Create menu and choose Dr REX Loop Player.

3. Click the Browse Patch folder on the Dr REX.

4. Browse to the Reason Factory Sound Bank folder, the Dr REX Drum Loops subfolder, and the Dub subfolder.

5. Double click on the file Dub15_DubHead_eLab.rx2.

6. Set the left locator point (L) to 1.1.1 and the right locator point (R) to 17.1.1.

7. On the Dr REX device, click the To Track button to print 16 bars into the sequencer.

8. Because this loop is one bar long, there are 16 different groups printed in the sequencer (see Figure 6.17). To begin deleting every other group of data, first click the Selection tool.

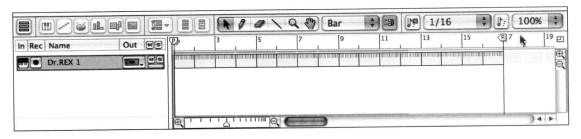

Figure 6.17
The sequencer before groups are deleted.

9. Click the second group in the track to select it (see Figure 6.18).

10. Open the Edit menu and choose Delete. Alternatively, press the Delete or Backspace key on your keyboard. Your sequencer should look like the one in Figure 6.19.

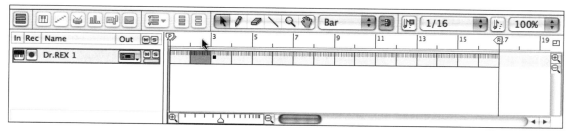

Figure 6.18

Using the Selection tool, select the second Group of data.

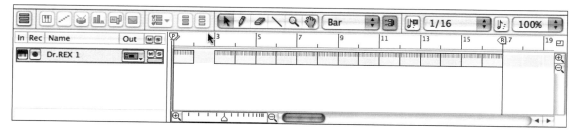

Figure 6.19

The sequencer with the second group of data deleted.

11. Click the Eraser tool to select it.

12. Click the group stretching from bar 4 to bar 5 to delete it.

13. Continue deleting every other group of data in the Dr REX track. When you are finished, the sequencer should look like the one in Figure 6.20.

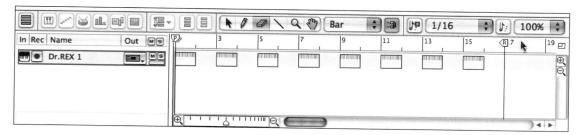

Figure 6.20

The sequencer with every other group of data deleted.

Resizing Groups

Groups appear onscreen with a small square handle on the right side. You can click this handle and drag left or right to make the group shorter or longer. If you make a group shorter, the small red vertical lines representing the events that were originally inside the group will appear, and can be individually edited and selected (see Figure 6.21).

Figure 6.21

Shortening a group reveals small red vertical lines that represent notes/events.

Groups cannot overlap. If you were to try to elongate a group such that it overlapped the next group, the overlapping part of the second group would be combined into the first group.

To practice resizing groups, do the following:

1. Open the file ResizingGroup.rns on the included CD-ROM. You'll see a Dr REX device loaded with a patch and the groups of data printed in the sequencer, shown in Arrange mode.

2. Click the Selection tool.

3. The first group of data in the Dr REX track in the sequencer is two bars long. Suppose, however, that you want to use only the first half of the group, making it one bar long and deleting the second half of the data. To begin, click the group to select it.

4. Click the square handle on the right side of the group.

5. Drag the handle to the left so that the group ends at bar 2 instead of bar 3. This reveals the red events between bar 2 and 3 so that your sequencer looks like the one in Figure 6.22

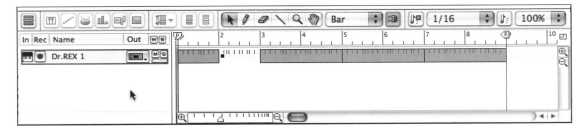

Figure 6.22

Resizing a group to be shorter.

6. Change the Snap Value setting to Bar.

7. Using the Selection tool, draw a box around the red events between bar 2 and bar 3.

8. Open the Edit menu and choose Delete or press the Delete or Backspace key on your keyboard. You now have a one-bar group from bar 1 to bar 2, a blank slate from bar 2 to bar 3, and then the original two-bar group from bar 3 to bar 5.

9. Next, combine all this into a four-bar group. Using the Selection tool, click the square handle at the end of the one-bar loop and drag it to the right all the way to bar 5. The result will be that this one-bar loop merges with the blank bar between bar 2 and bar 3 and the original two-bar group from bar 3 to bar 5, as shown in Figure 6.23.

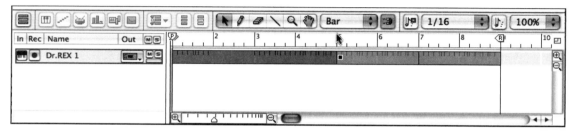

Figure 6.23

Elongating a group to merge several groups together.

Using the Change Events Dialog Box

Reason's Change Events dialog box, shown in Figure 6.24, contains some special editing features that can be used to alter selected events. Using this dialog box, you can transpose a melody to a different key, adjust the velocity, scale the tempo, and alter notes. This section looks at the different ways you can use the Change Events dialog box, launched from the Edit menu, when editing your compositions.

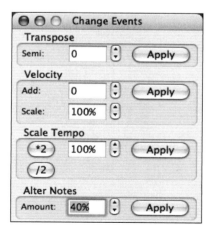

Figure 6.24

The Change Events dialog box.

Transposing Notes

There may be times when you want to hear how a song sounds in a different key, or when your singer can't quite hit the high note and needs to use a key that better suits her voice. Whatever the reason, it is easy to transpose notes using Reason's Transpose function. Use the Selection tool to highlight the notes or groups of data you want to transpose use the Change Events dialog box to choose the number of semitones to shift the data up or down, and then click the dialog box's Apply button.

To practice transposing a melody, do the following:

1. Open the file Transpose.rns on the included CD-ROM.

2. Click the Piano track in the sequencer.

3. Switch to Edit mode so you can see the Key and Velocity lanes.

4. Suppose you want to ask a violinist play on top of this melody, which is in the key of E minor, but her favorite key is D minor. To accommodate her, you'll need to transpose the notes down two semitones, from E to D# and from D# to D. To begin, click the Selection tool.

5. Draw a box around all the notes to highlight the entire selection. Alternatively, click somewhere in the Key lane, open the Edit menu, and choose Select All, or press Command+A(Mac) or Ctrl+A(PC).

6. Open the Edit menu and choose Change Events to open the Change Events dialog box.

7. Transpose this melody from E to D involves a shift of two semitones. For this reason, you'll need to click the down arrow next to the dialog box's Semi field twice to enter a value of −2.

8. Click the Apply button. All the notes are shifted down two semitones, as shown in Figure 6.25.

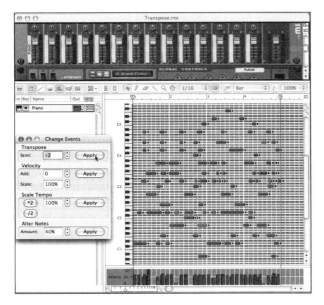

Figure 6.25

The data in the sequencer after transposing down two semitones.

133

Changing Velocity

Suppose you recorded a part but later realized you played all the notes just a little too softly. Or suppose some of the notes in the sequencer are being triggered too intensely and you would like to hear them at about half their velocity. The Change Events dialog box allows you to make these types of changes on a group of selected notes or events.

You adjust a note's velocity in much the same way as transposing notes. First, select all the notes or groups of notes whose velocity you want to adjust. Next, add or subtract a fixed amount of velocity or scale the velocity by a certain percentage. A note's velocity can range from 1 to 127, with a value of 1 producing the softest sound.

To practice adjusting the velocity using the Change Events dialog box, do the following:

1. Open the file AdjustVelocity.rns on the included CD-ROM.

2. Click the Piano track in the sequencer.

3. Switch to Edit mode so you can see the Key and Velocity lanes.

4. Listen to this melody; you'll probably notice that the notes are all struck a bit too hard, and that the melody would be nicer if it was a bit more delicate.

5. Click the Selection tool.

6. Draw a box around all the notes to select them. Alternatively, open the Edit menu and choose Select All.

7. Open the Edit menu and choose Change Events.

8. In the Velocity section, type 50% in the Scale field, and click the Apply button. As shown in Figure 6.26, the velocity for all the selected notes is cut in half.

Scaling the Tempo

Suppose there's a section of your song where you would like to put on the brakes and hear everything in half time. Unfortunately, Reason does not allow you to automate the master tempo. You can, however, use the Change Events dialog box's Scale Tempo section to process your MIDI data to achieve the same effect. Specifically, you can change your song's tempo by a certain percentage. There are handy shortcuts for doubling or halving the tempo of the selected MIDI data; I like to experiment with layering a melody on top of itself at different speeds to create interesting juxtapositions.

To get used to working with the Scale Tempo function, do the following:

1. Open the file ScaleTempo.rns on the included CD-ROM. Notice the blue group of data in the Bells track.

2. Open the Create menu and choose to create a new sequencer track.

134

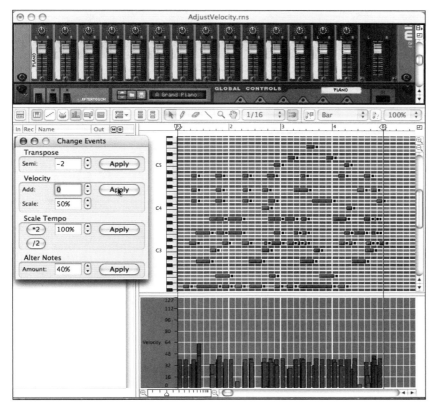

Figure 6.26
The sequencer after the
velocity is scaled by 50%.

3. To map the new, unassigned sequencer track's data to trigger the Combinator device to
   which the Bells track is assigned, click the new track's Out column and choose Bells, which
   is the name of the Combinator device (see Figure 6.27).

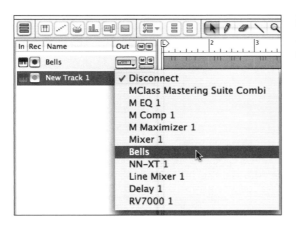

Figure 6.27
Assign the newly created sequencer track to trigger the
same SubTractor as the Bells track.

4. Click the Selection tool.

5. Hold down Option(Mac) or Alt(PC) key, click the green group in the Bells track, and drag this group to the sequencer track to duplicate it, dropping it right at the beginning of bar 1. Your sequencer should now look like the one in Figure 6.28.

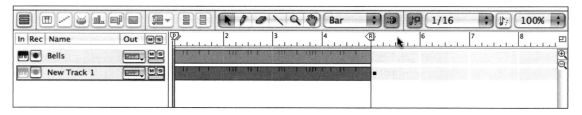

Figure 6.28

The sequencer after the group from the Bells track is copied to the new sequencer track.

6. Click the Switch to Edit View button.

7. Click the New Track 1 sequencer track. Notice the notes in the Key lane that make up this group of data.

8. Using the Selection tool, draw a box around all the notes to select them.

9. Open the Edit menu and choose Change Events.

10. In the Change Events dialog box, click the /2 button in the Scale Tempo section to set the amount to 50% (see Figure 6.29).

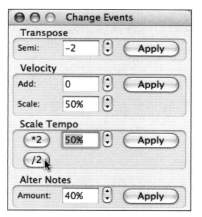

Figure 6.29

Setting the scale tempo to 50%.

11. Click the Apply button to cut the tempo of the four bars of notes in half, making the melody eight bars long (see Figure 6.30).

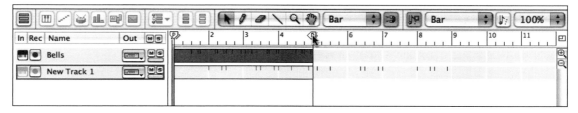

Figure 6.30
Data in the new sequencer track after the tempo has been halved.

12. Change the right locator point (R) to 9.1.1 and click Play to hear how these eight bars sound.

> **Tip**
>
> The key to making this technique work well is to use a fairly sparse melody, with only a few complementary notes. For example, choose only three or four notes that comprise a chord as I did here, using only the notes that comprise C major.

Altering Notes

The Alter Notes function essentially shuffles the notes you have selected. This function alters the pitch, length, and velocity of the selected notes, using only values that already exist in the selected notes. For example, if you have a song written in the key of B minor and you highlight the notes and apply the Alter Notes function, the reshuffled notes will still be in the same key, although the melody itself may be rearranged. The higher the percentage you select for the Amount setting, the more shuffling will occur. Applying a smaller percentage will retain more of the original melody.

This function is very useful for spicing up your melodies. It is also great for experimenting with REX loops. If you select some notes on a Dr REX track and use the Alter Notes function, you will create variations without losing the timing and rhythmic feel of the loop.

To practice altering notes, do the following:

1. Open the file AlterNotes.rns on the included CD-ROM.

2. Click the Dr REX track in the sequencer. It is loaded with the REX loop Dub15DubHead_080_eLab.rx2.

3. Set the left locator point (L) to 1.1.1 and the right locator point (R) to 5.1.1.

4. Click Preview to hear what this dub beat sounds like at this tempo.

5. On the Dr REX device itself, click To Track to print the data to the sequencer.

6. Switch to Edit mode so you can see the REX lane. You'll see four bars of this REX loop, which contains a total of 17 slices.

7. Click Play to listen.

8. Click the Selection tool.

9. Draw a box around slices 10–17 in these four bars (see Figure 6.31).

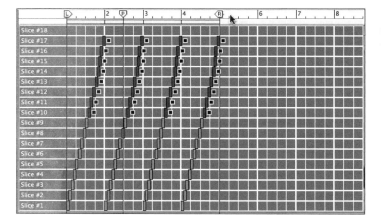

Figure 6.31

Selecting slices 10–17 for these four bars of the REX loop.

10. Open the Edit menu and choose Change Events to open the Change Events dialog box.

11. Type **50%** in the Amount field in the Alter Notes section and click the Apply button. Because this is a random function, each time you perform it you will achieve a different effect; nonetheless, your sequencer should look something like the one in Figure 6.32.

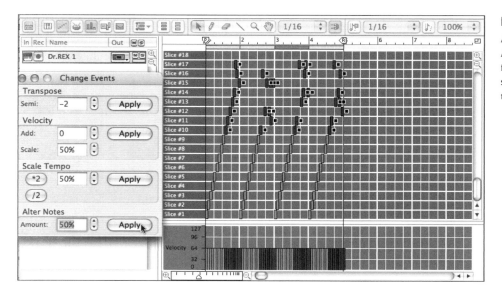

Figure 6.32

Applying the Alter Notes function on slices 10–17 in the REX lane.

7

Recording and Editing Velocity and Controller Data

This chapter looks at the tools and techniques Reason offers for recording and editing velocity and controller data. Reason gives you the ability to record parameter automation, which allows you to record a mix or a performance and then go back and further refine the data. In this chapter you will examine the various ways to edit velocity data, learn how to set up the sequencer to record controller data, and look at the tools Reason offers for editing that data.

The Velocity Lane

When you record a musical performance in Reason, by default you record both the note data and the velocity data. Note data includes which key was played and when, while the velocity data documents how hard each note was struck, with values ranging from 1–127. The velocity data is displayed in the Velocity lane (see Figure 7.1). Higher velocity values correspond to taller, darker red bars, while smaller velocity values appear shorter and lighter in color—more pink. Each note has a corresponding bar in the Velocity lane.

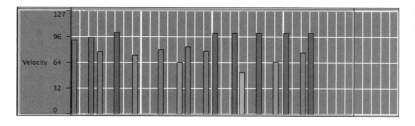

Figure 7.1
The Velocity lane.

Resizing the Velocity Lane

Reason allows you to resize the height of the Velocity lane. That way, if you are doing some detailed micro-editing, you can give yourself more space to work; conversely, if you need a bit more space elsewhere on your screen, you can shrink the Velocity lane accordingly. To resize the Velocity lane, just position your mouse pointer on the boundary between the Velocity lane and the lane above it; the cursor turns into an icon with arrows pointing up and down (see Figure 7.2). Click and hold down the mouse button to grab the boundary, and drag up or down to resize the height of the Velocity lane. This comes in handy if you are working on a complicated drum fill or are finessing the subtle dynamics of a particular section of a melody.

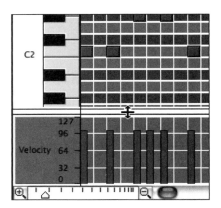

Figure 7.2

Rolling your mouse pointer over the boundary changes the pointer icon, letting you know that you can now resize the height of the Velocity lane.

Editing Velocity Data

If you draw in notes using the Pencil tool, they will by default have a velocity of 100. This velocity might work fine for some scenarios, but most of the time it can leave the music feeling a little stiff, without any dynamics. Reason offers you several ways to edit the velocity values after notes are entered into the sequencer. One is to use the Line tool to create velocity ramps and curves; another is to use the Pencil tool to create irregular curves.

Creating Velocity Ramps with the Line Tool

The Line tool (see Figure 7.3) enables you to edit the velocity of several different notes at once. To use the Line tool, simply click in the Velocity lane, hold down the mouse button, and drag to create a line. When you release the mouse button, the velocity values of any notes included between the point where you clicked to the point where you dragged will be adjusted to the point where the line intersected them, creating a velocity ramp. This trick comes in handy for creating a drum roll or a fill, and is also great for creating a bass or keyboard line that slowly grows in intensity.

Figure 7.3
The Line tool.

To practice using the Line tool to create a velocity ramp for a drum fill, do the following:

1. Open the file VelocityRamp.rns on the included CD-ROM.

2. Click the Redrum track in the sequencer.

3. Click the Switch to Edit Mode button to reveal the Drum lane and Velocity lane.

4. As you can see, notes have been printed into the Drum lane and that there is a fill just before bar 5, but the velocity of all these notes is the same. To make the fill more effective, create a velocity ramp; begin by clicking the Line tool.

5. Place your mouse pointer over the boundary between the Velocity lane and the Drum lane; it will change to a double-arrowed icon. Click and drag up to increase the viewing area of the Velocity lane.

6. Let's focus on the notes between bar 4 and 5—in particular, the second half of the bar where a bunch of Clp_Xfile1.wav 1/32 notes create a machine-gun effect (see Figure 7.4). In the Velocity lane at the beginning of these notes, starting at bar 4 beat 3, click with the Line tool near the bottom at a very low velocity. Then, holding your mouse button down, drag upward and to the right, releasing near the top of the Velocity lane to create an upward-sloping line (see Figure 7.5). The velocity of all the notes under this line is affected, creating an upward-slanting ramp. Your sequencer should look like the one in Figure 7.6.

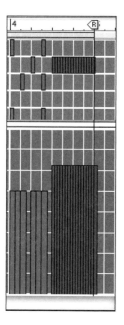

Figure 7.4
A series of 1/32 notes for the sound Clp_Xfile1.wav in the Drum lane.

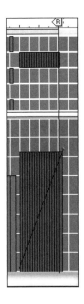

Figure 7.5

Using the Line tool to create an upward-sloping velocity ramp.

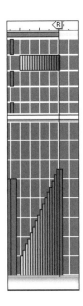

Figure 7.6

When the mouse button is released, the velocity of all notes across the range is affected.

Using the Pencil Tool to Create Irregular Curves

The Line tool is great for creating regular, smooth velocity ramps, or for making all the notes have the same velocity by drawing a straight line. There will be times, however, when you want to create a more *irregular* curve—that is, a curve that is not straight. The Pencil tool (see Figure 7.7) is ideal for this job.

Figure 7.7

The Pencil tool.

To use the Pencil tool to draw in a velocity curve, just click the tool and then click anywhere in the Velocity lane where there are notes. If a note's velocity is currently below where you clicked in the Velocity lane, it will immediately jump up to the position you clicked. If you click and hold down the mouse button and draw in a curve, the velocity of each note will jump to where the Pencil tool intersected the note in the Velocity lane. This allows you to draw in fancy curves or change the velocity of one note at a time.

Sometimes you may find it useful to adjust the velocity of certain notes only. If these notes reside inside a crowded cluster of activity, however, doing so may be tricky. For example, suppose you have a Redrum part programmed and printed to the sequencer and you want to adjust the velocity of the hi hats only. It would be no problem if no other parts were programmed yet, but chances are you will have to navigate around the kick drum, snare drum, and so on. To do this, first choose the Selection tool and then click on the notes whose velocity you wish to adjust. Hold down the Shift key to select multiple notes. Switch back to the Pencil tool. If you hold down the Shift key while you draw in the Velocity lane with the Pencil tool, only the selected notes will be affected.

To practice drawing in velocity curves with the Pencil, as well as holding down the Shift key to adjust selected notes only, do the following:

1. Open the file VelocityPencil.rns on the included CD-ROM.

2. Click the Malström track in the sequencer.

3. Click the Switch to Edit Mode button to reveal the Key lane and Velocity lane.

4. As shown in Figure 7.8, the track has a scattering of notes with a velocity of 100. To draw in some velocity variations for these notes, first click the Pencil tool.

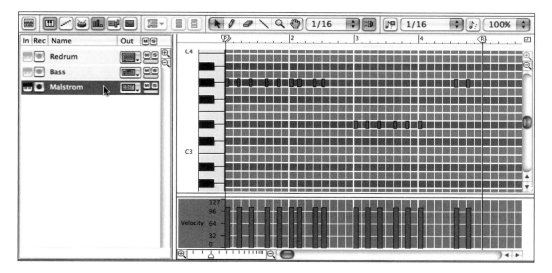

Figure 7.8

Notes on the Malström track, all with a Velocity value of 100.

5. Draw a curve that is like a sine wave, starting with a higher velocity and then dipping down and back up again for the first cluster of G#3 notes.

6. Repeat step 5 for the second cluster of D#3 notes. Your sequencer should look like the one in Figure 7.9.

7. To practice using the Shift key to adjust only selected notes, let's create an alternating pattern for the open hi hats OH_Xfile1.wav. To begin, click the Redrum track in the sequencer. Notice that except for the velocity ramp at the end, all the notes in the Drum lane have a velocity of 100.

143

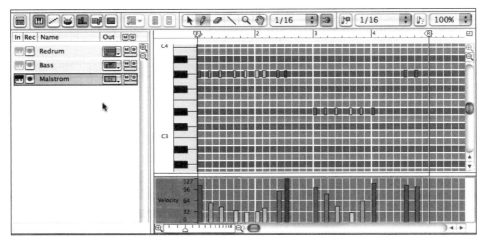

Figure 7.9

The sequencer after drawing in a velocity curve on the Malström track with the Pencil tool.

8. Click the Selection tool.

9. Draw a box around all the notes on the channel OH_Xfile1.wav to select them (see Figure 7.10).

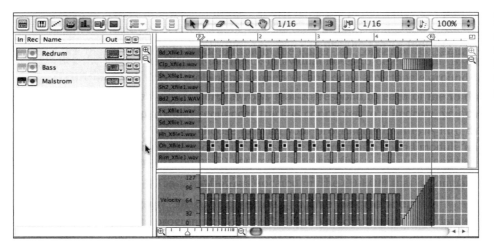

Figure 7.10

All the notes on the OH_Xfile1.wav channel are selected.

10. Click the Pencil tool.

11. Holding down the Shift key, draw in the Velocity lane with the Pencil tool such that the velocity alternates and every other open hi hat note has a smaller velocity. By holding down the Shift key, you ensure that only the open hi hats will be affected; all the values for the other notes in the Drum lane will remain intact. When you are finished, your sequencer should look like the one in Figure 7.11.

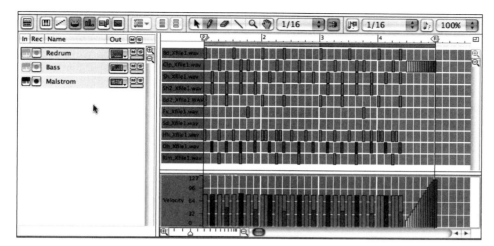

Figure 7.11
The sequencer after you've altered the velocity of the notes with the Pencil tool while holding down the Shift key to ensure that only the selected notes are affected.

Recording Controller Data

Reason allows you to record and edit controller data (that is, knob movements, fader movements, button on/offs, and such). Indeed, almost every parameter on every device can be automated. Parameters that can be automated appear with a blue downward-pointing arrow when you enter Remote Override Mapping mode, which is covered this section. You can map the parameters to a knob or fader on your MIDI controller and then record and capture every detail of your performance, which you can then go back and edit. Here you'll take a look at the basics of setting up remote MIDI mapping, recording controller data, and then editing this data.

Remote Basics

Propellerheads has developed the Remote protocol to handle incoming MIDI input from control surfaces in Reason. Remote is essentially a mapping system that identifies your connected MIDI controller and then automatically maps the most logical parameters for each Reason device to the various knobs and faders on your controller. You can also override these automatic mappings to create your own custom configurations. Reason supports most major MIDI hardware, and Propellerheads is constantly updating and adding new devices as they become available.

Remote Override Mapping

Reason's Remote feature automatically maps parameters to knobs and faders on your MIDI controller. You may discover, however, that you would rather map a particular knob to a different parameter than what it is set up to control by default. Reason's Remote Override Mapping feature allows you to customize your own mappings.

After your MIDI controller is properly selected and enabled, you are ready to map the various device parameters to corresponding controls on your MIDI controller. The best way to understand this process is by doing an exercise, so do this one on remote override mapping. You will need to have a MIDI controller connected and properly set up in order to do this exercise.

> **Note**
>
> You learned about setting up your MIDI controller in Chapter 3, "Playing MIDI Notes," so I won't go over it again here.

1. Open the file RemoteOverrideMapping.rns on the included CD-ROM.

2. Click the Malström track in the sequencer.

3. Open the Options menu and choose Remote Override Edit Mode (see Figure 7.12). When you do, Reason becomes slightly grayed out with little blue arrows on all the parameters that can be mapped. The standard pre-mapped parameters of the device appear with a little yellow and black circle on them, as shown in Figure 7.13. (Note that for this example, I am using an Evolution UC-33e. Depending on which device you are using and how many knobs and sliders you have available, your screen may look different.)

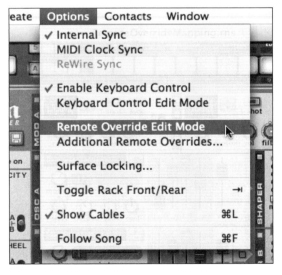

Figure 7.12

Open the Options menu and choose Remote Override Edit mode.

4. Place your mouse pointer over one of the yellow and black circles to view a tool tip indicating which control on the control surface is mapped to that parameter.

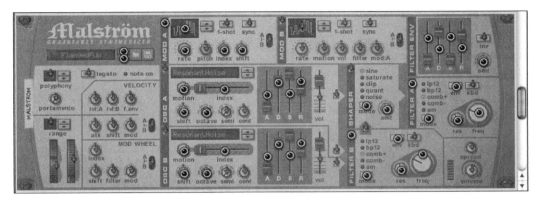

Figure 7.13

In Remote Override Edit mode, Reason becomes grayed out. Unmapped parameters appear with a blue arrow, while unmapped parameters feature a yellow and black circle.

5. For this example, create a custom mapping for the attack (A) of the filter envelope (Filter Env), which is located in the upper-right corner of the Malström. To begin, double-click the filter envelope attack fader; it turns into a spinning yellow lightning bolt (see Figure 7.14).

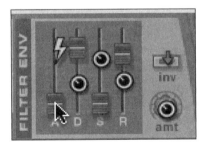

Figure 7.14

Double-clicking a parameter in Remote Override Edit mode turns it into a spinning yellow lightning bolt, indicating that it is waiting for you to move it.

6. Move a knob or fader on your MIDI controller. As soon as you do, the yellow lightning bolt stops spinning and turns into an orange lightning bolt, indicating that the parameter has been mapped to the knob or fader on your controller that you just moved (see Figure 7.15).

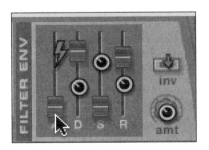

Figure 7.15

When the parameter is mapped, the lightning bolt stops spinning and turns from yellow to orange.

147

7. Click the Options menu and choose Remote Override Mapping Mode to de-select it.

8. Move the knob or fader on your MIDI controller that you just mapped; you will see that it now controls the attack of the filter envelope.

Recording Parameter Automation

Now that you have set up your MIDI controller and properly mapped the knob on your device to the parameter you wish to control, you can record the automation into the sequencer. In this example, you'll automate the attack of the filter envelope. Here's how:

1. The file RemoteOverrideMapping.rns should still be open, with the filter envelope's Attack parameter mapped to the knob on your MIDI controller from the previous exercise. To begin recording the automation, click the Malström track's Record button in the sequencer. It will turn red, indicating that it is record enabled (see Figure 7.16).

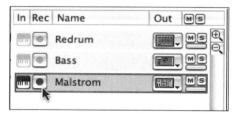

Figure 7.16
Record-enable Malström track.

2. Record-enable the Global Record button in the Transport.

3. Turn off the Loop function.

4. You are now ready to record controller automation. Start with the Attack parameter at a low value, and then use the knob on your MIDI controller to increase the value between bars 2 and 3 and bars 4 and 5.

5. Click Stop. The Attack fader of the filter envelope now appears with a green highlight, letting you know it has been automated (see Figure 7.17).

Figure 7.17
The Attack fader of the filter envelope now appears highlighted in green, indicating that it is automated.

9. Click the Show Controllers in Track button in the toolbar (see Figure 7.18). Your sequencer should look something like the one in Figure 7.19, although it will differ slightly depending on how you moved the parameter in your performance.

Figure 7.18
The Show Controllers in Track button.

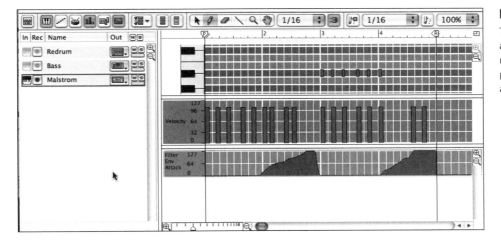

Figure 7.19
The sequencer after you've recorded your parameter automation.

Recording Parameter Automation for the Mixer 14:2

To record parameter automation for the mixer, do the following:

1. First, create a new sequencer track by opening the Create menu and selecting Sequencer Track (see Figure 7.20). This creates a blank, unassigned track in the sequencer.

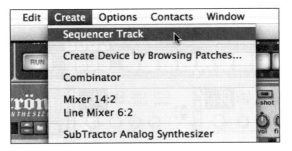

Figure 7.20
Create a new sequencer track.

2. Choose the mixer in the Out column for this new track (see Figure 7.21).

149

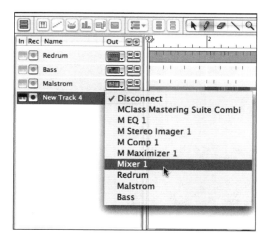

Figure 7.21
Assign new blank sequencer track to the mixer.

3. Record-enable the sequencer track assigned to the mixer.

4. Enable the Global Record button.

5. You are ready to capture your mix. If you have a MIDI controller with faders, you can assign them to control the various channels of the mixer and record your hands-on mix.

The beautiful thing about recording your mix in real time as opposed to drawing it in is that you get that hands-on feel, which gives your music personality, emotion, and uniqueness. You can then go back and refine your captured performance, tweaking it to sound just the way you want it to.

Editing Controller Data

After you have recorded controller data into the sequencer, you can go back and edit it, making further refinements and subtle adjustments. Controllers are displayed and edited in the Controller lane, which is further divided into subtracks for each automatable parameter of that particular device. In this section you will take a look at the editing tools available for working with controller data, as well as some of the techniques for moving, duplicating, and deleting sections in the Controller lane.

Showing/Hiding the Controller Lane

The Controller lane has subtracks for every parameter of that sequencer track's corresponding device. You can view all these subtracks or you can display only those that are actually automated. To see the Controller lane in Arrange mode, click the Show Controller Lane button in the toolbar (see Figure 7.22).

Now that you can see the Controller lane in the sequencer, you can click either the Show Device Controllers button (see Figure 7.23) to display all the subtracks or the Show Controllers in Track button (see Figure 7.24) to display only the automated controllers. Alternatively, you can display individual controllers by clicking the Controllers button (see Figure 7.25), which opens a menu of all the available parameters for that particular device.

Figure 7.22
The Show Controller Lane button.

Figure 7.23
The Show Device Controllers button.

Figure 7.24
The Show Controllers in Track button.

Figure 7.25
Clicking the Controllers button opens a menu that enables you to display a particular parameter.

Finally, you can show a parameter in the Controller lane by right-clicking (PC) or Ctrl-clicking (Mac) that parameter on the device itself and then choosing Edit Automation from the menu that appears. If you hold down the Option (Mac) or Alt (Windows) key and click a parameter on a device panel in the device rack above the sequencer, the sequencer will switch to Edit mode and display the Controller lane of the first sequencer track connected to this device, showing the specific automation subtrack for the parameter you selected.

Drawing and Editing Controller Parameters

As you learned earlier in this chapter, you can record the automation of controller parameters. Alternatively, you can draw the information directly into the Controller lane from scratch. However you enter the information into the Controller lane, you can edit it using the Pencil tool and the Line tool.

Note

You can draw in continuous curves by leaving the Snap to Grid function turned off, or you can draw and edit to the nearest Snap Value position if Snap to Grid is turned on. When using the Line tool, you can restrict your movement to the horizontal only by holding down the Shift key when you are drawing.

Before you enter any data into a parameter subtrack in the Controller lane, the track will display a 'Not Automated' notice. Figure 7.26 shows the pan automation for track 1 of the mixer; because no data has yet been entered, the 'Not Automated' notice is displayed.

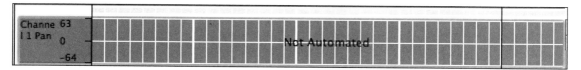

Figure 7.26

If no data has been entered, the subtrack in the Controller lane for that particular parameter will appear with the words "Not Automated," as it does here with the pan parameter of track 1 on the mixer.

The best way to learn how to edit controller data is with an example or two, so let's do a few exercises on drawing in Controller data—one using the Line tool and one using the Pencil tool.

1. Open the file DrawingControllers.rns on the included CD-ROM. You see four tracks of data in the sequencer: Redrum, Bass, Malström, and Mixer.

2. In this example, let's draw in an automation curve for the panning of the Malström track in the sequencer, which is track 3. To begin, on the mixer in the rack, right-click (PC) or Ctrl-click (Mac) the pan of track 3 (the Malström track) and choose Edit Automation from the menu that appears (see Figure 7.27). This switches the sequencer to Edit mode and shows the Channel 3 Pan subtrack in the Controller lane of the mixer track. It currently says "Not Automated."

3. Let's use the Line tool to draw in a continuous pan curve for this four-bar loop. To begin, click the Line tool.

4. Ensure that the Snap to Grid function is turned off by making sure the button with the magnet on it is not illuminated.

5. Click the 0 value in the center of the pan track at bar 1, hold down the mouse button, drag all the way to the top, and release; the pan should have a value of 63 at bar 2. Your sequencer should look like the one in Figure 7.28.

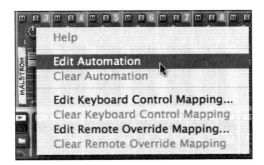

Figure 7.27

Right-click or Ctrl-click the pan for track 3 of the mixer and choose Edit Automation.

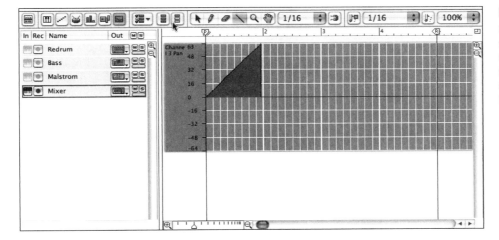

Figure 7.28

Use the Line tool to draw the first part of the pan curve from bar 1 to bar 2.

6. Using the Line tool, click the value 63 at bar 2, hold the mouse button down, drag all the way to the bottom value at bar 4, and release; the pan should have a value of −64 at bar 4. Your sequencer should look like the one in Figure 6.29.

7. Click the value −64 at bar 4, hold down the mouse button, drag so that pan has a value of 0 at bar 5, and release. Your sequencer should look like the one in Figure 7.30, with an alternating pan effect over this four-bar range for the Malström track. The pan dial on the mixer is now outlined with green, letting you know that it is an automated parameter (see Figure 7.31).

Let's do another exercise to get a feel for using the Pencil tool to draw in controller data. Again using the file DrawingControllers.rns on the included CD-ROM, which has four tracks of data in the sequencer—Redrum, Bass, Malström, and Mixer—let's use the Pencil tool to draw in a mod wheel automation for the Malström device.

1. Click the Malström track on the sequencer to select it.

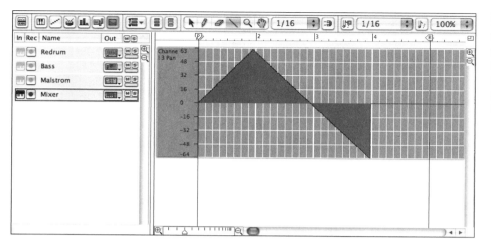

Figure 7.29

Use the Line tool to draw the second part of the pan curve from bar 2 to bar 4.

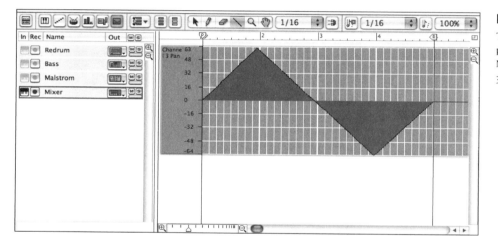

Figure 7.30

The finished pan curve for Malström track 3 on the mixer.

Figure 7.31

The pan dial on the mixer is outlined in green, indicating that it is an automated parameter.

2. Click the Controllers button (see Figure 7.32) and choose Mod Wheel from the menu that appears (see Figure 7.33). This opens the Mod Wheel subtrack in the Controller lane of the Malström sequencer track.

Figure 7.32
Click the Controllers button.

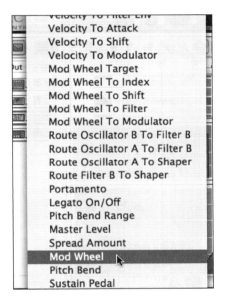

Figure 7.33
Choose Mod Wheel from the menu that appears.

Velocity To Filter Env
Velocity To Attack
Velocity To Shift
Velocity To Modulator
Mod Wheel Target
Mod Wheel To Index
Mod Wheel To Shift
Mod Wheel To Filter
Mod Wheel To Modulator
Route Oscillator B To Filter B
Route Oscillator A To Filter B
Route Oscillator A To Shaper
Route Filter B To Shaper
Portamento
Legato On/Off
Pitch Bend Range
Master Level
Spread Amount
Mod Wheel
Pitch Bend
Sustain Pedal

3. Click the Pencil tool.

4. Click the button with a magnet on it to turn on the Snap to Grid function. (The button should be illuminated.)

5. Change the Snap Value setting to 1/4 (see Figure 7.34).

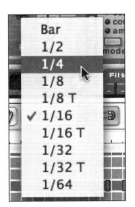

Figure 7.34
Change the Snap Value setting to 1/4.

Bar
1/2
1/4
1/8
1/8 T
✓ 1/16
1/16 T
1/32
1/32 T
1/64

6. Draw an upward-sloping staircase for the mod wheel. To do so, click near a 0 value at bar 1, hold down the mouse button, and drag up toward a value of 127 at bar 3. Because the Snap to Grid function is turned on, you will create a sort of staircase effect (see Figure 7.35).

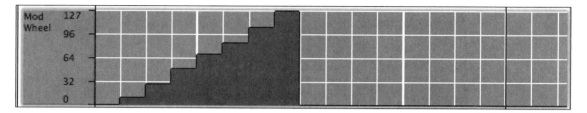

Figure 7.35
Drawing in parameter data with Snap to Grid function enabled creates a series of discrete jumps.

7. For the second half of these four bars, try drawing a continuous curve with the Pencil tool. First, turn off the Snap to Grid function by clicking the button with a magnet on it. It should not be illuminated.

8. Click near a 0 value at bar 3, hold down the mouse button, and drag an upward curve shape toward the 127 value at bar 5. The Malström sequencer track's Mod Wheel parameter subtrack in the Controller lane should look like the one in Figure 7.36.

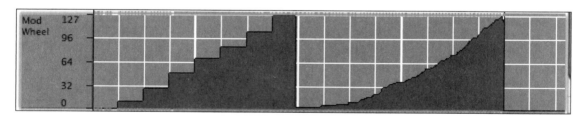

Figure 7.36
Mod wheel automation.

Selecting, Moving, Copying, and Deleting Data in the Controller Lane

Data can be copied, deleted, and moved in the subtracks of the Controller lane. For example, say you have drawn in a great curve that you want to repeat throughout the song or that you want to use to automate a different parameter. Reason lets you do both.

The first step is to use the Selection tool to highlight the stretch of the Controller lane you want to work with. I find it useful to use the Snap to Grid function for copying a selection so that it has an even, exact length. Just click the appropriate parameter subtrack of the Controller lane and, holding down the mouse button, drag to the right, releasing at the end of the section (see Figure 7.37).

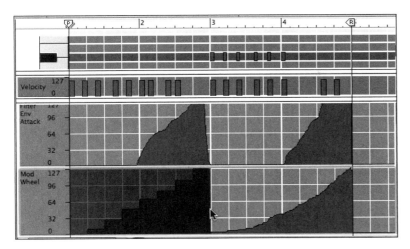

Figure 7.37
Selecting the first two bars of the Mod Wheel parameter automation.

To copy the selected area, either open the Edit menu and choose Copy (see Figure 7.38) or press Ctrl·C (PC) or Command·C (Mac). After you have copied the selected area, move the position marker (P) to the location where you want to paste the data, open the Edit menu, and choose Paste (see Figure 7.39) or press Ctrl+V (PC) or Command+V (Mac).

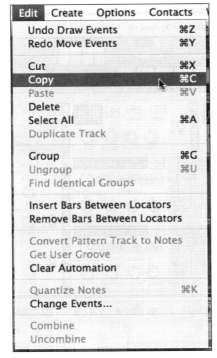

Figure 7.38
Choose Copy from the Edit menu.

Figure 7.39

Choose Paste From the Edit Menu.

To move a section of controller data, simply select it, click the selection, and, holding down the mouse button, drag it to a different position on the same controller track.

> **Note**
>
> If you hold down the Option key (Mac) or the Alt key (PC) while moving the data, a little green plus sign appears to let you know that you are actually duplicating it rather than simply moving it.

To delete a section of controller data, select the area you want to delete, open the Edit menu, and choose Delete or press the Backspace or Delete key on your keyboard. Alternatively, use the Eraser tool to delete the data. If the Snap to Grid function is on, then clicking the data with the Eraser tool will delete the range determined by the Snap Value setting. Thus, if you have a value of one bar selected as your Snap Value, clicking the Eraser on the Controller lane will erase batches of data one bar in length at a time. Clicking and dragging the Eraser tool across the lane will delete sections in multiples of the Snap Value setting. If Snap to Grid is not active, you can delete data unconstrained by the grid.

Note, however, that you can't delete *all* the controller data with these methods. There will always be at least one value remaining in the Controller lane for this parameter. To completely remove all the data from the Controller lane, you must clear the automation. To do so, simply right-click (PC) or Ctrl-click (Mac) the desired parameter and choose Clear Automation from the menu that appears (see Figure 7.40). This removes all data for this particular parameter from the sequencer.

Figure 7.40

Select Clear Animation from the menu that appears after you right-click or Ctrl-click a parameter.

Copying Data Between Different Controller Subtracks

In Reason, you can copy controller data from one parameter and apply it to another parameter. For example, suppose you have drawn a nice fade curve on one subtrack that you would like to use to modulate a different parameter on another device altogether. To do so, follow these steps:

1. Open the file CopyingControllerData.rns on the included CD-ROM.

2. Click the Mixer track; you'll see a zig-zag curve for the Pan parameter on track 3.

3. Click the Selection tool.

4. Select bar 1 to bar 5 of this Controller lane. Your sequencer should look like the one in Figure 7.41.

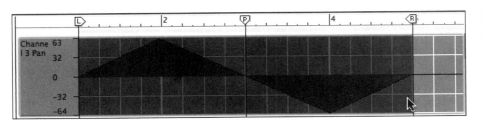

Figure 7.41

Select the first four bars of track 3's Pan parameter in the mixer's Controller lane.

5. Next, use this same curve for the panning of the hi hat on channel 8 of the Redrum. To begin, click the Redrum track in the sequencer so that it displays the Redrum device in the rack above it.

6. Right-click (PC) or Option-click (Mac) the Pan dial of the Redrum channel 8 and choose Edit Automation from the menu that appears (see Figure 7.42). This opens the Redrum track in the sequencer, switching it to Edit mode and displaying the channel 8 Pan parameter in the Controller lane (see Figure 7.43).

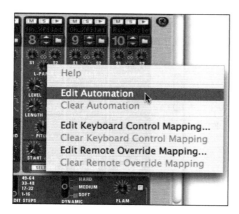

Figure 7.42

Right-click or Option-click the parameter and choose Edit Automation from the menu that appears.

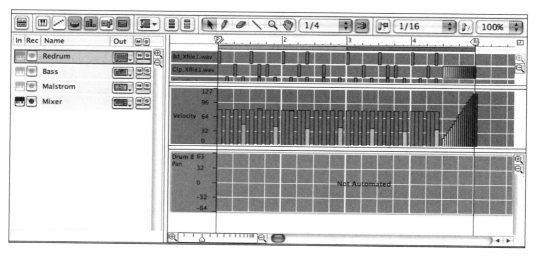

Figure 7.43

Choosing Edit Automation displays the parameter's Controller lane in the sequencer.

7. If the Position marker (P) is not already at position 1.1.1, grab it and move it there.

8. Open the Edit menu and choose Paste or press the Ctrl+V (PC) or Command+V (Mac) keyboard shortcut. Your sequencer should look like the one in Figure 7.44.

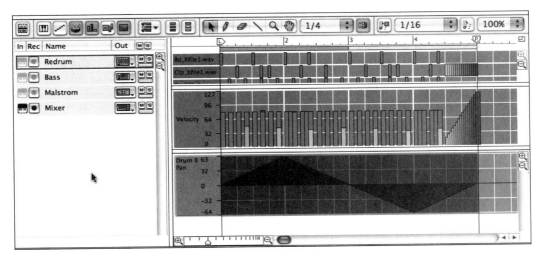

Figure 7.44

The sequencer after the curve has been pasted into the Redrum channel 8 Pan parameter in the Redrum Controller lane.

Copying Controller Data for Multiple Parameters

Reason allows you to copy data across several different subtracks of the Controller lane at a time. Holding down the Shift key and using the Selection tool allows you to highlight stretches of data on several different parameters at once. This becomes useful if you have mapped several different parameters to different controls on your MIDI device, and you have recorded a performance moving different knobs and faders at the same time. Perhaps there are moments across the subtracks that work well together, and you would like to copy and paste them into a different section of the song to repeat the sound.

To practice copying controller data for several parameters, do the following:

1. Open the file CopyingMultipleControllers.rns on the included CD-ROM; notice that you have eight bars of music.

2. Click the Switch to Edit Mode button.

3. Click the Malström track in the sequencer to select it. As depicted in Figure 7.45, you see two automated parameters in the Controller lane: the Filt Env Attack and Mod Wheel.

4. Copy the first two bars of data from both of these parameters and paste them at bar 5. To begin, click the Selection tool.

5. Select the data from bar 1 to bar 3 for the Filt Env Attack parameter. Holding down the Shift key, also select the data from bar 1 to bar 3 for the Mod Wheel parameter. Your sequencer should look like the one in Figure 7.46.

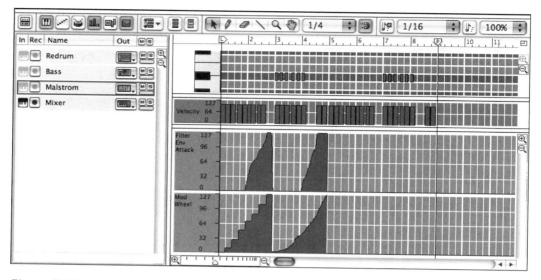

Figure 7.45

Two automated parameters in the Controller lane of the Malström track.

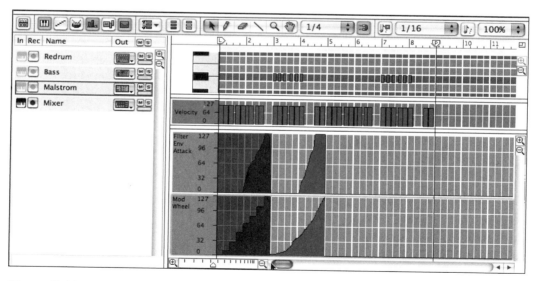

Figure 7.46

Selecting data in the Controller lane for both parameters from bars 1–3.

6. Open the Edit menu and choose Copy. Alternatively, press the Ctrl+C(PC) or Command+C (Mac) keyboard shortcut.

7. When you perform the Copy operation, the Position marker (P) jumps ahead to the end of the selection at bar 3. Grab the marker and move it to bar 5.

8. Open the Edit menu and choose Paste. Alternatively, press the Ctrl+V(PC) or Command+V (Mac) keyboard shortcut. Your sequencer should look like the one in Figure 7.47.

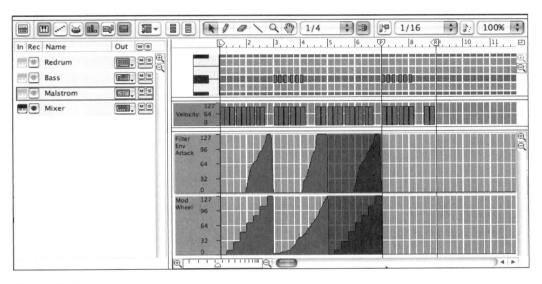

Figure 7.47

The sequencer after the copied data has been pasted at Bar 5 for the Malström track.

8 Quantization

Reason's Quantization function enables you to move recorded notes to (or closer to) exact note value positions. You can use quantization to tighten up a performance, correct mistakes, or simply change the rhythmic feel of your piece. Say, for example, that you played a bass line for a SubTractor and although you nailed the performance for the most part, there was a section in the middle where your timing was a little off. You can use Reason's Quantization function to fix this. You can also quantize your rhythm parts. Moreover, you can use the Get User Groove function to extract the feel of one melody or rhythm and then use the extracted feel to quantize a different part altogether. The creative application of the quantization tools is a vital part of getting the most out of the Reason sequencer. This chapter looks at the quantization tools, which are located in the upper-right corner of the sequencer (see Figure 8.1). It discusses their functionality, demonstrating how to quantize both beats and melodies. You will also look at Reason's Shuffle feature, used to give your music some swing.

The Quantization button   The Quantize Notes button

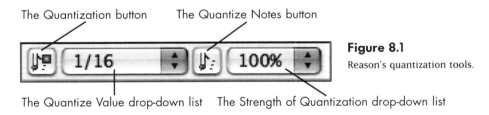

Figure 8.1
Reason's quantization tools.

The Quantize Value drop-down list   The Strength of Quantization drop-down list

The Quantize Value Setting

The first thing you do when quantizing is to select the notes you wish to quantize. The next step is to establish the value to which you want to quantize the notes. You choose this value from the Quantize Value drop-down list (see Figure 8.2). Options include Bar, 1/4, 1/8, 1/8T, 1/16, 1/16T, 1/32, 1/64, Shuffle, Groove 1, Groove 2, Groove 3, and User.

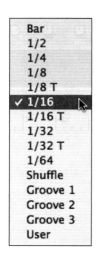

Figure 8.2
The Quantize Value drop-down list.

The first options are recognizable note values, as large as one bar and as small as a 1/64th note. There are even a few note values with triplets. Then there are options to quantize to three different default grooves, each with their own feel. The best way to figure out which groove works best for you is to experiment with them. Finally, the Quantize Value drop-down list contains a User option. Reason enables you to extract the groove or feel of a melody or rhythm, basically any particular selection of notes or REX slices, and then use that custom User groove as the Quantize Value for a different selection of notes. This is a powerful function that enables you to customize your production in a powerful way. Finally, there is a Shuffle option. You'll take a look at the User and Shuffle settings a little later in this chapter.

The Strength of Quantization Setting

After you have selected the notes you want to work with and established the Quantize Value setting, the next step is to adjust the Strength of Quantization setting (see Figure 8.3). This setting determines the degree to which the notes will be forced toward the selected note value on the grid. The available values are 100%, 90%, 75%, 50%, 25%, 10%, and 5%. If you select a value of 100%, all the selected notes will be forced precisely to the grid determined by the Quantize Value setting. Choosing smaller values enables you to retain some of the original feel of the part you are quantizing. Your best bet is to experiment with these percentages to figure out the best solution for each situation. Sometimes you may want a part to be more rigid—for example, with the kick and snare drums—while for other parts, perhaps with the keyboard melodies, you might want to retain a looser feeling.

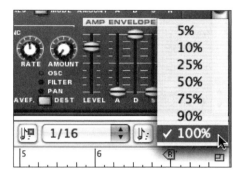

Figure 8.3

The Strength of Quantization drop-down list.

The Quantize Notes Button

Now that you have selected the notes, established the Quantize Value and Strength of Quantization settings, it is time to click the Quantize Notes button to actually quantize the material. The Quantize Notes button (see Figure 8.4) processes the selected notes and physically shifts their position on the grid according to the settings you selected.

Figure 8.4

The Quantize Notes button.

To familiarize yourself with the quantization procedure, do the following:

1. Open the file QuantizeDrums.rns on the included CD-ROM.

2. Click the Redrum track in the sequencer to select it.

3. Click the Switch to Edit Mode button. There are numerous notes in the Drum lane; listening to them, you hear that the drum part is quite sloppy and loose. Let's tighten the part up using quantization.

4. Select all the notes in the Drum lane either by drawing a box around them with the Selection tool or by choosing Select All from the Edit menu. Alternatively, use the Command+A (Mac) or Ctrl+A(PC) keyboard shortcut.

5. Select 1/16 from the Quantize Value drop-down list (see Figure 8.5).

6. Change the Strength of Quantization setting to 100% (see Figure 8.6).

7. Click the Quantize Notes button. Notice how the notes shift; your sequencer should look like the one in Figure 8.7.

167

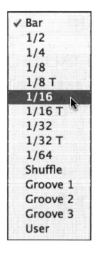

Figure 8.5

Select 1/16 from the Quantize Value drop-down list.

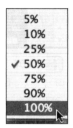

Figure 8.6

Change the Strength of Quantization setting to 100%.

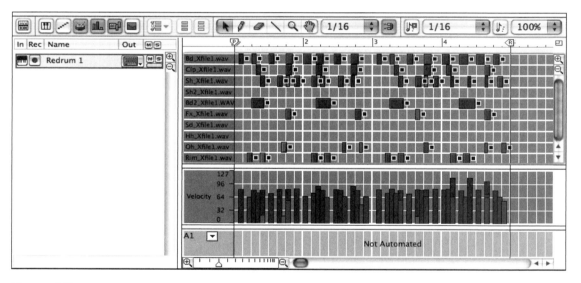

Figure 8.7

The Redrum track in the sequencer after quantization.

8. Click Play; you should hear a noticeable difference.

Now that you have tightened up the drum part, let's add a bass line to it and experiment with various values for the Strength of Quantization setting.

1. Open the file QuantizeBass.rns on the included CD-ROM.

2. Click the SubTractor bass track in the sequencer to select it.

3. Click the Switch to Edit Mode button. There are numerous notes in the Key lane; listening to them, you hear that the bass part is close, but was played in a little too loosely for this already-quirky drum part.

4. Select all the notes in the Key lane of the SubTractor bass track either by drawing a box around them with the Selection tool or by choosing Select All from the Edit menu. Alternatively, use the Command+A (Mac) or Ctrl+A(PC) keyboard shortcut.

5. Select 1/16 from the Quantize Value drop-down list.

6. Change the Strength of Quantization setting to 75%.

7. Click the Quantize Notes button. Notice how the notes shift.

8. Click Play. You should hear a noticeable difference. That said, setting the Strength of Quantization value to 75% did not make this part completely complementary with the drums.

9. Open the Edit menu and choose Undo Quantize Notes (see Figure 8.8). Alternatively, press Command+Z(Mac) or Ctrl+Z(PC).

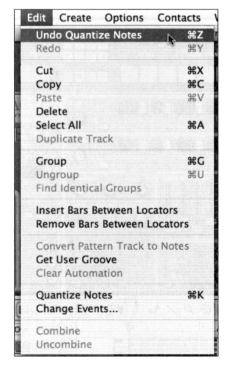

Figure 8.8

Select Undo Quantize Notes from Edit menu.

10. Change the Strength of Quantization value to 90%.

11. Click the Quantize Notes button.

12. Click Play and listen; notice that it still does not feel completely right. Again open the Edit menu and choose Undo Quantize Notes or press Command+Z (Mac) or Ctrl+Z (PC) to undo the quantization.

13. Change the Strength of Quantization setting to 100%.

14. Click the Quantize Notes button.

15. Click Play and listen; the part sounds better.

This example is a good lesson in how to experiment with different values until you find the one that best suits the material you are working with. If I had played this part in a bit better you might have been able to get away with a smaller percentage value for the Strength of Quantization setting, but because the original performance was a bit sloppy, using a strength of 100% yielded the best results.

Groove 1, Groove 2, Groove 3

The Quantize Value drop-down list features options called Groove 1, Groove 2, and Groove 3. These are built-in rhythmic patterns that you can use to quantize to. If you select one of these from the Quantize Value list and then click the Quantize Notes button, the selected notes will be moved toward the note position in the groove pattern, creating a different feel.

To get the hang of quantizing to one of these grooves, do the following:

1. Open the file QuantizeGroove123.rns on the included CD-ROM.

2. Click the Switch to Edit Mode button. There are numerous notes in the Drum lane; listening to them, you hear that this drum part is very sloppy.

3. Select all the notes in the Drum lane either by drawing a box around them with the Selection tool or by choosing Select All from the Edit menu. Alternatively, use the Command+A (Mac) or Ctrl+A(PC) keyboard shortcut.

4. Choose Groove 1 from the Quantize Value drop-down list (see Figure 8.9).

5. Change the Strength of Quantization setting to 100%.

6. Click the Quantize Notes button. Notice how the notes shift.

7. Click Play. You should hear a noticeable difference. That said, the Groove 1 setting doesn't resolve the problems with this rhythm, so let's undo our actions.

8. Open the Edit menu and choose Undo Quantize Notes. Alternatively, press Command+Z(Mac) or Ctrl+Z(PC).

9. Change the Quantize Value setting to Groove 2.

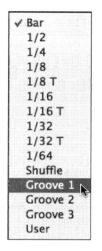

Figure 8.9
Select Groove 1 from the Quantize Value drop-down list.

10. Click the Quantize Notes button.

11. Click Play and listen to the results. Notice that it still does not feel completely right. Again open the Edit menu and choose Undo Quantize Notes or press Command-Z (Mac) or Ctrl-Z (PC) to undo the quantization.

12. Change the Quantize Value setting to Groove 3.

13. Click the Quantize Notes button.

14. Click Play and listen; the part sounds better. Your sequencer should look like the one in Figure 8.10.

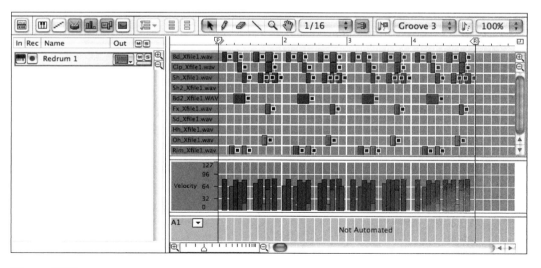

Figure 8.10
The sequencer after quantizing with the Groove 3 Quantize Value setting.

By understanding this concept, you lay the groundwork for understanding the custom User setting, which enables you to use the Get User Groove function to extract the rhythmic feel from one groove and then apply it to another when you quantize any selected group of data, be it REX slices or notes in the Key lane or Drum lane. You can extract the rhythmic feel of a REX loop or one of your own recorded performances, whatever rhythm is inspiring you. You'll explore the Get User Groove function later in this chapter.

Shuffle

One of the Quantize Value selections is Shuffle, which adds a touch of swing to your music. The amount of shuffle you add when quantizing is determined by the Pattern Shuffle dial in the lower-right corner of the Reason Transport (see Figure 8.11). Turning this dial to the right adds more shuffle, making the swing more pronounced. For subtle shuffle effects, I usually choose something in the 10–30% range. If I'm going for an over-the-top effect, I may set this in the 60–80% range. Clearly, you'll adjust this setting to your own taste, so you will want to experiment with the various values and see how they affect the selected material.

Figure 8.11
Use this dial to set the desired amount of shuffle.

To practice quantizing the REX slices of a Dr REX player using the Shuffle Quantize Value setting, do the following:

1. Open the file QuantizeRexShuffle.rns on the included CD-ROM.

2. Click the Dr REX 1 track in the sequencer to select it.

3. Click the Switch to Edit Mode button.

4. Click the To Track button on the Dr REX device in the rack (see Figure 8.12) to print the REX data in the sequencer from bar 1.1.1 to bar 9.1.1.

Figure 8.12
Click To Track to print the REX notes to the sequencer.

5. Notice the individual REX slices printed in the REX lane. Click Play and listen to this drum part as it is, straight out of the box.

6. Use the Shuffle Quantize Value setting to give this part a little swing. To begin, select all the notes in this REX lane either by drawing a box around them with the Selection tool or by choosing Select All from the Edit menu. Alternatively, press Command+A (Mac) or Ctrl+A(PC).

7. Click Shuffle in the Quantize Value drop-down list (see Figure 8.13).

Figure 8.13
Choose Shuffle from the Quantize Value drop-down list.

8. In the lower-right corner of the Reason Transport, turn the Pattern Shuffle dial to the right so that it has a value of 100 (see Figure 8.14).

Figure 8.14
Turn the Pattern Shuffle dial to 100.

9. Set the Strength of Quantization value to 100% (see Figure 8.15).

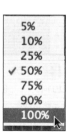

Figure 8.15
Change Strength of Quantization setting to 100%.

10. Click the Quantize Notes button. All the REX slices are slightly shifted, and your sequencer should look like the one in Figure 8.16. You can hear the difference; there is now a more pronounced swing to the beat.

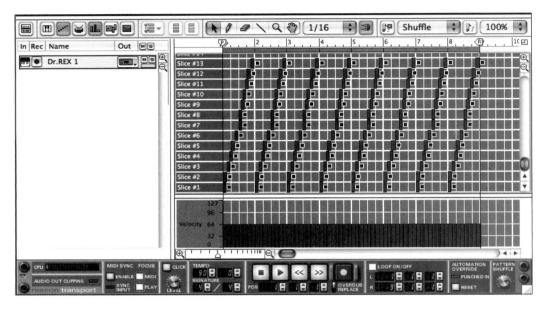

Figure 8.16
The sequencer, quantized with the Shuffle option.

User

Reason enables you to capture your own custom user grooves and use them to apply quantization. You can capture the groove of a melody that you have played in yourself or you can extract the feel of your favorite REX loop. Then you select another group of notes or REX slices and apply the custom User quantization. Using this function is an incredible way to personalize your productions, giving them your own unique flavor and differentiating yourself from all the other producers making music with Reason.

The best way to demonstrate how to use this function is with an exercise. Try the following:

1. Open the File UserGroove.rns on the included CD-ROM; you'll see a Redrum track and a SubTractor bass track. Let's extract the groove from a REX loop and use it to quantize the Redrum drum notes.

2. Open the Create menu and choose Dr REX Loop Player.

3. Click the Browse Patch button.

4. Choose Reason Factory Sound Bank, select Dr REX Drum Loops, choose Glitch, and choose the file Glt04_120.

5. Set the left (L) and right (R) locator points to 1.1.1 and 5.1.1, respectively.

6. Click the To Track button to print the REX slices into the sequencer (see Figure 8.17).

Figure 8.17
Click the To Track button to print the REX notes into the sequencer.

7. Click the Dr REX track in the sequencer, and then click the Switch to Edit Mode button.

8. Click the Selection tool.

9. Draw a box around all the notes in the REX lane.

10. Select Get User Groove from the Edit menu (see Figure 8.18)

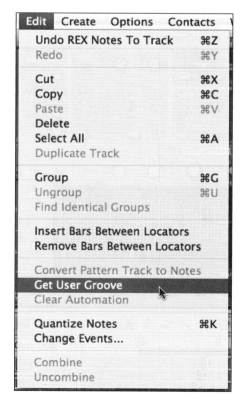

Figure 8.18
Select Get User Groove from the Edit menu.

11. Now that you have extracted the feel of this REX loop, use it to quantize the Redrum part. To begin, click the Redrum track in the sequencer.

12. In the Drum lane, draw a box around all the notes or choose Select All from the Edit menu. Alternatively, use the Command+A(Mac) or Ctrl+A(PC) keyboard shortcut.

13. Select User from the Quantize Value drop-down list (see Figure 8.19).

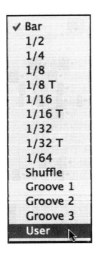

Figure 8.19

Select User from the Quantize Value drop-down list.

14. Change the Quantize Strength setting to 100%.

15. Click the Quantize Notes button. This forces all the notes in the Drum lane of the Redrum track to have the same feel as the REX loop you printed in the sequencer. Your sequencer should look like the one in Figure 8.20.

This was an example of how you can extract the feel of a REX loop and apply it to a Redrum part that you have played in by hand. You can also extract the feel of a part that you played in yourself and then use that for your Quantize Value setting. For example, say you like the dubby feel of the SubTractor bass part from the previous example. In the same way that you selected the REX slices in the REX lane, you could select the notes in the SubTractor bass track and choose Get User Groove from the Edit menu to extract the feel of this melody. You can now use this to quantize another melody. In this manner, you can play in a rhythm, extract its vibe, and then apply it to other parts. You can quantize REX slices, notes in the Key lane, or notes in the Drum lane. Some producers like to play in their own rhythms just so they can extract them and quantize with them. This is a great feature of Reason; it gives you the power to make your productions all your own.

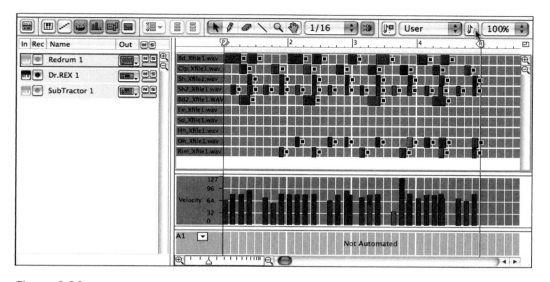

Figure 8.20

The sequencer after quantizing with the User groove.

Pulling Everything Together

When crafting a track, producers often start with the drums and bass, first getting the rhythm section dialed in tight. Next they might add the melodic elements such as keyboard and guitar parts, and then any pads and sound-design elements to spice things up. Again, there is no right or wrong order with recording the various parts; you just have to find an approach and a workflow that works for you. After you have recorded all the various components that comprise your song—regardless of how the data was entered and in what order—the next step is to mix them all together.

Mixing is a skill that requires some time and effort to master. You must learn to train your ears to recognize the different frequencies and to hear where the various elements are clashing. Sometimes these issues can be resolved through the use of EQing and panning, while other times it has to do with setting appropriate volume levels for the various parts. A good mix should sound crisp, not muddy, and unless you are deliberately going for something different sonically, you should be able to hear all the different parts of the song clearly and distinctly. Whatever sonic effect you're shooting for, learning to master the subtle art of mixing will make the difference between your tracks sounding professional and sounding amateurish.

> **Note**
> You might opt to muddy things up in your mix if, for example, you are creating a wall of sound to build up the tension before breaking things down. Alternatively, you might blur the lines between the different parts rather than going for something clear and distinct if you want several parts to mysteriously weave in and out of each other.

Automating Your Mixes

Now that you have all the components that comprise your song committed to the sequencer, it's time to mix them together, giving your song the necessary dynamics and setting the levels appropriately so that all the pieces fit nicely. Some parts may need to be louder during the chorus, but then pulled back in the verses. Perhaps you want to ease in a big ambient pad sound so that it slowly increases, building the energy of the track up and up until it reaches a critical point and you drop the hammer with a sick beat. Whatever the case, whatever you are working on, Reason enables you to automate your mixes by using either a MIDI controller or a mouse. You'll take a look at both methods now.

Automating Your Mixes with a MIDI Controller

Although you can use the mouse to record your mixer automation in Reason, most people prefer the hands-on feel they get from using a MIDI controller. The first step when automating a mix with a MIDI controller is to map all the appropriate mixer parameters to knobs and faders on the controller. By default, Reason maps these automatically to the most logical controls. As you learned in Chapter 7, "Recording and Editing Velocity and Controller Data," you can override these settings and create your own custom mappings.

When choosing a MIDI control surface, you'll want to consider what your needs are. If you are buying a keyboard, how many octaves do you need? Are you okay working with a two-octave, 25-note keyboard, or do you need four octaves and 49 keys or even an 88-key full-length model with weighted keys? If you plan to program beats with Reason, you might want a device with trigger pads. Knobs and sliders are great for mixing and creating filter sweeps on synths. There are many options out there, each with different configurations of sliders, faders, keys, pads, and buttons. Personally, I like to use a device that incorporates all these features, so I picked up the M-Audio Axiom 49 (see Figure 9.1), which features four octaves of keys with aftertouch, eight trigger pads, a set of faders, knobs, and buttons, and a set of transport controls.

Figure 9.1

The M-Audio Axiom 49 MIDI controller. (Photo Courtesy of M-Audio.)

After you have selected a MIDI controller and have everything set up the way you want it, go ahead and take a pass recording your every move as you mix the various components of your song together in real time. When you finish recording, you can go back through the sequencer and finesse your mix, using the Pencil tool and Line tool to make adjustments to the recorded performance.

To get used to the process, do the following:

1. Open the file AutomateMix.rns on the included CD-ROM. You'll see several instruments and a mixer, with data recorded in the sequencer.

2. To automate the mixer, the first thing you need to do is create a new sequencer track and then assign it to the mixer. To begin, open the Create menu and choose Sequencer Track (see Figure 9.2). A new unassigned track is created in the sequencer.

Figure 9.2
Choose Sequencer Track from the Create menu.

3. Click the new track's Out menu and choose the mixer (see Figure 9.3).

4. Before you do any automation, click play and listen; notice the broken beat drum pattern on the Redrum track.

5. Add a little EQ to help this part stand out in the mix. Click the EQ button on track 1 of the mixer to enable the EQ section; a red light should appear (see Figure 9.4).

6. To bring out the percussion parts on the high end, turn the Treble knob on track 1 to 26 (see Figure 9.5).

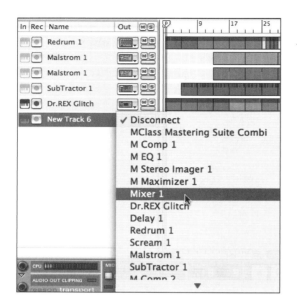

Figure 9.3

Assign the new sequencer track to the mixer

Figure 9.4

Turn on the EQ for track 1 of the mixer.

Figure 9.5

Turn up the treble on track 1 to 26.

7. When the SubTractor bass on track 2 kicks in at bar 5, it's a little weak in the mix. To boost it, bring its volume level to 70 (see Figure 9.6).

> **Note**
>
> Notice in Figure 9.6 that on the mixer, the bass track is labeled "EQ 1 Left." That's because the mono output from the SubTractor is going through a compressor and then through an EQ effect before going into the mixer. By default, the mixer track is named after the last device in the chain.

Figure 9.6
Turn up the volume of the bass track to 70.

8. Automate the Dr REX Glitch track, a subtle, glitchy percussion part, so that it works as an accent on the beats. First, map this track's volume slider to the appropriate fader on your MIDI controller. To begin, open the Options menu and choose Remote Override Edit Mode (see Figure 9.7).

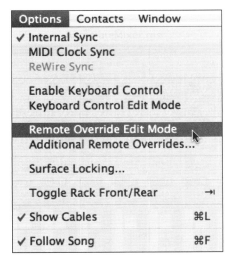

Figure 9.7
Choose Remote Override Edit Mode from the Options menu.

9. The mixer appears grayed out, with blue arrows on all the parameters. Double-click the blue arrow on the Dr REX Glitch track's Volume slider on the mixer; the arrow turns into a spinning yellow lightning bolt (see Figure 9.8).

10. Move the slider on the MIDI controller that you will use to automate this parameter. The onscreen Volume slider now appears with an orange lightning bolt, indicating that it has been mapped (see Figure 9.9).

Figure 9.8
Double-click the blue arrow on the Dr REX Glitch track's Volume slider. The arrow turns into
a spinning yellow lightning bolt, indicating that the parameter is waiting to be mapped.

Figure 9.9
After you move a fader on Your MIDI controller, the lightning bolt turns orange,
indicating that the parameter has been mapped.

11. You are ready to record the automation of this track on the mixer. Click the Record button
    on the New Track 6 track in the sequencer and enable the Global Record button (see
    Figure 9.10).

12. Click the Play button, move the volume fader up and down while recording a pass for the
    first 32 bars. Click the Stop button when you're finished.

13. Click the Switch to Edit Mode button.

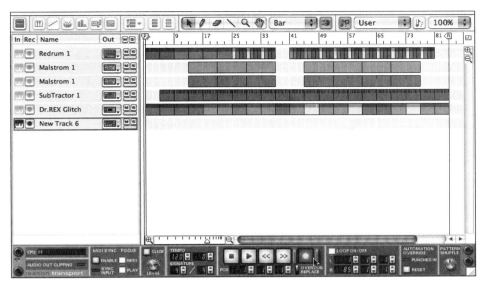

Figure 9.10

Enable the Record button on New Track 6 and the Global Record button.

14. With New Track 6 selected, you should now see the recording of your automation perform-ance. It will correspond to the moves you made with the fader and should look something like Figure 9.11.

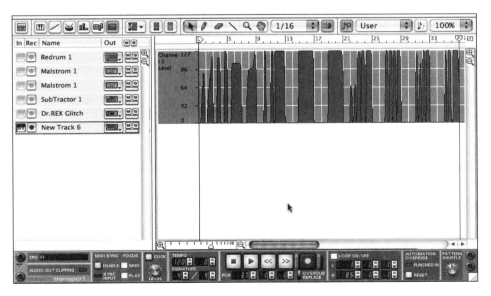

Figure 9.11

The automated fader in the sequencer track.

Automating Your Mixes with a Mouse

In addition to using a MIDI controller to automate your mixes, you can also use a mouse—although many people prefer the hands-on feel of a MIDI control surface. Nonetheless, if you are working on the road and do not have a controller with you, or if you need to do something quickly and setting up a control surface isn't worth the trouble, you can use the mouse to record your adjustments to these controls in real time and then go back over them to edit them further. This is actually a great way to develop a rough guideline for your mix; you can revisit it later, using the Pencil tool and the Line tool to further finesse the values.

> **Note**
>
> In fact, you can use your mouse to record automation for any parameter on any track in your sequencer as long as that track is record enabled. For example, suppose you want to record a filter ride on a synth or the panning on a channel on the Redrum. To do so, you use the same technique as when automating a parameter on the mixer. After you have record-enabled the sequencer track that you have assigned to the mixer and you have enabled the Global Record button, you can then click play and start recording your fader adjustments, using the mouse to control them.

Editing Mixer Automation Data

After you have recorded your mix and committed all your automation data into the Reason sequencer, you can go back and edit this controller data just like you did in Chapter 7. This mixer automation data is standard-issue controller data; as such it can be cut, copied, pasted, and deleted in the same manner as controller data associated with the various instruments. Specifically, you edit this data in the sequencer with the Pencil tool and the Line tool, finessing your performance and making any necessary adjustments. Similarly, you can automate the parameters on the various effect devices, perhaps mapping a knob on your MIDI controller to adjust the feedback of a digital delay and then perhaps ride that effect throughout the song to create dubby echo effects at the appropriate place. After you have recorded your automation performance, it appears in the sequencer as standard controller data, ready to be further revised with all the powerful tools available to you in Reason.

Mastering

To achieve the best sound possible with your productions, you should incorporate a mastering suite at the very end of the chain before your audio is routed out of the Reason hardware interface and out of the physical outputs of your audio interface. Although mastering doesn't necessarily pertain to the MIDI sequencer (unless you are automating the various parameters of the mastering devices, such as the EQ for example), the process of properly finishing your song is quite important to sequenced music. At the end of the day, you want your sequenced music to sound as good as possible, so it makes sense to get familiar with some of the mastering tools that are available to you.

Mastering is a skill that requires a certain amount of practice, but Reason comes with some factory settings that do a fantastic job. For example, Reason's MClass Mastering Suite Combinator (see Figure 9.12) comes with a number of presets for various types of music, including Acoustic, Dance, Hard Rock, Hip Hop, Pop, and more. I create electronic music, so I often find myself using the Kompakt setting, after the exquisite German electronic record label of the same name. You should experiment with the various settings and discover the ways in which they affect your music; they serve as a great starting point for mastering your tracks.

Figure 9.12

The MClass Mastering Suite Combinator.

Using the MClass Mastering Suite Combinator in Reason 3

One of the big improvements in Reason 3 is the inclusion of the Combinator device—in particular, the MClass Mastering Suite. This chain of devices includes the MClass Compressor, MClass Equalizer, MClass Stereo Imager, and MClass Maximizer. Used together, these high-quality effects combine to make a fantastic suite for mastering your audio output. Adding one of these devices just before the audio gets routed out the hardware interface, right after your master output from the mixer, will help make your music sound loud and clear. It does help to learn how to tweak the settings to get the most out of this mastering suite, but you will find that just adding the device to the chain and using one of the default settings will go a long way in helping take your tracks reach the next level.

In this day and age, almost every record company, music supervisor, agent, and manager will have certain expectations when it comes to the quality of the submissions they receive. If you don't take the time to master your work either by doing it yourself or by getting it done professionally, you put yourself at a serious disadvantage. That said, it is important to communicate with your label or with your production team to make sure you know what they expect from you.

> **Note**
>
> If your song will be part of a compilation, the label releasing the comp will likely hire a professional mastering engineer, which means they will probably want to receive your music without any compression or brick-wall limiting. You want to be careful to not overdo it with the compressor or maximizer so your music will retain a nice dynamic range. Overly compressed music sounds like the work of an amateur to most people, so exercise a certain amount of restraint when it comes to adding compression.

To practice inserting a mastering suite between the output of a mixer and the Audio Out in the Reason Hardware Interface, do the following:

1. Open the file InsertMasteringSuite.rns on the included CD-ROM. You'll see a number of devices routed into the mixer, which is connected directly to the Audio Out section of the Reason Hardware Interface.

2. Insert the MClass Mastering Suite. To begin, click the Reason Hardware Interface on the very top of the rack to select it.

3. Open the Create menu and choose MClass Mastering Suite Combi (see Figure 9.13).

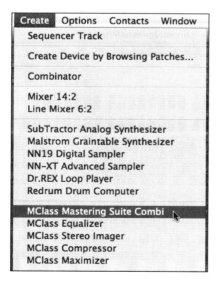

Figure 9.13
Select MClass Mastering Suite Combi from the Create menu.

4. Because you selected the Reason hardware interface in step 2, the mastering suite should be automatically routed between the mixer and the Audio Out. To ensure that it is in fact properly routed, press the Tab key on your keyboard to flip around to the back. As you can see in Figure 9.14, it is routed correctly.

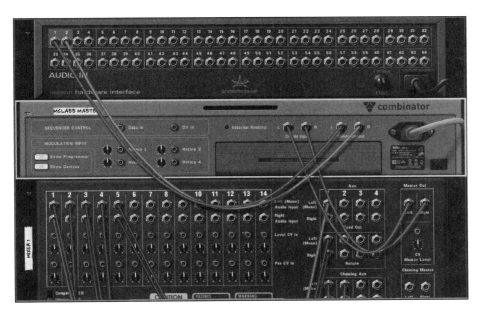

Figure 9.14

The MClass Mastering Suite is automatically routed between the mixer output and the Audio Out on the Reason Hardware Interface.

Note

If for some reason the mastering suite is not routed properly, you can adjust it manually by clicking the ports on the back of any device in Reason and connecting the cables by hand with the mouse. Routing audio in Reason can be a lot of fun, and it provides a platform for some serious experimentation.

Mastering with Scream 4

In earlier versions of Reason, before the advent of the MClass Mastering Suite Combinator, Scream 4 (see Figure 9.15) served as an excellent tool for beefing up your sound. In particular, Scream 4's Warm Saturation preset (see Figure 9.16) includes the excellent Compress Master setting. Acting like an old analog tape compressor, Scream 4 can really give your tracks a nice, warm feeling. Even though the new MClass Mastering Suite is the bomb, I still find myself using the Scream 4 device fairly often in my mixes.

Figure 9.15

Scream 4 is great for mastering.

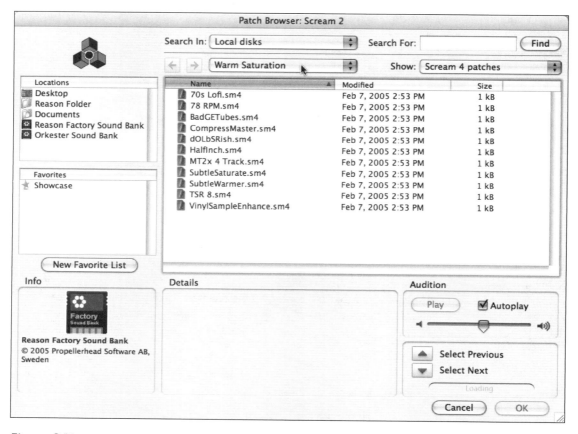

Figure 9.16

Warm Saturation presets for Scream 4, including the Compress Master setting.

Reason Hardware Interface

Along the top of the Reason rack is the Reason Hardware Interface and the Audio Out section. If you press the Tab key to flip around to the back of the Reason rack, you will see 64 different inputs on the Reason Hardware Interface listed as Audio In (see Figure 9.17). In this picture, you see the output of the Mixer 14:2 getting routed first into the inputs of the MClass Mastering Suite and then into outputs 1&2 of the Audio In section of the Reason hardware interface. As I mentioned, it's generally a good idea to add a mastering suite as the last element in your chain of devices before routing into the Audio In section of the Reason Hardware Interface.

Figure 9.17
The back of the Reason Hardware Interface's Audio In section.

If you are working with Reason in ReWire mode, using Reason's instruments and devices as sound modules as Reason is slaved to another application, you would use these other channels on the Audio In section to set up separate streams. Thus, you can separately route different devices to different pairs of outputs, bringing them into your host application on separate channels and keeping the audio distinct. For example, you can bring the drums on one pair, the bass on another, keys on another, and so on. That way, you can use other plug-ins in your host application to process these individual audio parts separately.

If you have a sound card with more than two outputs, you can also choose to route the audio out the separate physical outputs on your hardware. For example, you might want to route one device out into a physical hardware effect such as a delay pedal or Kaoss pad. Using these other outputs enables you to control what audio signals get routed out to these effects. If you are doing a live show and you are working with a great sound guy, he might want to receive the various instruments as separate channels on his board so he can have more control over the overall mix. For example, he might want the bass separate from the drums or the Rhodes so he can adjust the level; if you are sending him only one mixed output, there is less he can do with it. Sometimes, however, you might want to keep tighter control of your levels, in which case it might make sense to only send a stereo mix. It really depends on the venue and the situation, not to mention your level of trust in the live sound engineer.

Exporting

After you have recorded all your parts, set the proper levels of the mix, and added the appropriate mastering devices, the next step is to export the mixed-down track as a single audio file. Using Reason, you can export files in one of two ways: the Export Loop as Audio File command or the Export Song as Audio File command.

The Export Song as Audio File Command

After you have everything set just the way you like, it's time to bounce down the song as a single stereo file. When you choose the Export Song as Audio File command from the File menu (see Figure 9.18), Reason renders the stereo output from outputs 1&2 of the Audio Out device across the range determined by the beginning of the song and the end marker (E).

Figure 9.18

Choosing the Export Song as Audio File command.

Note

If you set the end marker (E) right at the very end of the music, the song will stop abruptly at that position. If you have a lush chord with a long decay and lots of delay or reverb on it, however, you probably want it to slowly fade out. In that case, be sure to give yourself enough time after the last notes in the sequencer for the sound to properly decay. I usually click play, listen, and visually determine where the sound is all the way out by watching the sequencer, noting the location of the position marker (P) when the sound fades all the way down to silence. Then, I move the end marker (E) to the right as need be. It is better to give yourself a bit of extra room at the end than have it abruptly stop out. That said, you don't want *too* much extra time at the end; otherwise, you will have an awkward silence between your tracks if you are burning them to CD.

The Export Loop as Audio File Command

Choosing the Export Loop as Audio File command from the File menu (see Figure 9.19) also renders the master output from Outputs 1&2 down as a stereo file, but only bounces the audio down across the range determined by the left and right locator points (L) and (R). There is no difference in the quality of the rendering; the only difference between the Export Loop as Audio File and Export Song as Audio File operations is the markers used to determine the range.

Figure 9.19

Choosing Export Loop as Audio File from the File menu.

> **Note**
>
> I often use the Export Loop as Audio File command, however, because I find it easier to set the L and R locator points for my song's in and out.

The Export Loop as Audio File function is also great for generating a bunch of loops. I love to work with Reason as my beat-construction machine; I often load up a Redrum device with a bunch of sounds and then experiment with a number of different patterns, bouncing them out as short two- or four-bar loops, which I then work with when composing or experimenting live. Reason is an incredible tool, and there are so many different ways to use it; part of the fun is discovering all the wonderful ways you can make it work for you.

Entering Song Information and Publishing Your Song

After you have created your masterpiece, Reason gives you the option of saving information with the song such as the song's title, your email address, and more. You can even select an image to be associated with the song. To enter this information, open the appropriate song and then click on the File menu and choose Song Information (see Figure 9.20) or press the Control+I (Mac) or Ctrl+I (PC) keyboard shortcut. This launches the Song Information dialog box shown in Figure 9.21. Enter your information in the fields provided and click OK.

Figure 9.20

Select Song Information from the File menu.

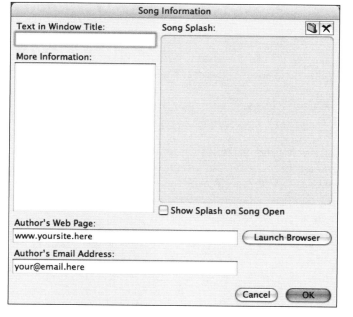

Figure 9.21

The Song Information dialog box contains fields for entering personal information, including your web site's URL and your email address.

After you have entered all your song information, you can publish your song. This saves the song as a Reason Published Song (RPS) file, as indicated by the .rps file extension. RPS files can be made available for download by others—for example, via the Propellerheads web site (http://www.propellerheads.se). To publish your song, open the File menu and choose Publish, as shown in Figure 9.22.

Figure 9.22

Select Publish Song from File menu.

Closing Remarks

I hope this book has been a useful resource for you, helping you to harness the power of the Reason sequencer. Now it is time for you to dive in and experiment, exploring different techniques and approaches to making music and finding a workflow that suits you best. Remember to enjoy the process, and don't be afraid to try something new. Have a lot of fun with Reason! Thank you.

Index

V

W

Y

Z

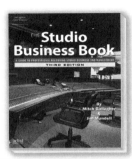

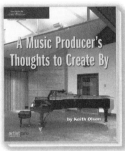

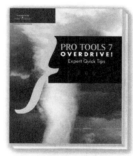

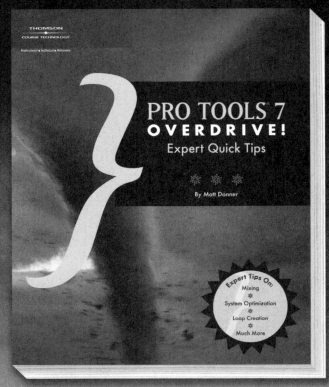

Get S.M.A.R.T.

Serious Music and Audio Recording Techniques

Introducing the *S.M.A.R.T. Guide* Series from Thomson Course Technology PTR/ArtistPro Publishing.

The *S.M.A.R.T. Guide* series is designed to provide a comprehensive, up-to-date education on classic and modern techniques for professional audio production. Providing a logical progression of knowledge, if the entire series is followed from the first through the sixth title, readers will gain a well-rounded and clear understanding of audio recording.

Readers also have the option of focusing on a title to learn one vital aspect of the audio recording process. Each title presents concepts in clear readable language, includes numerous full color screenshots and pictures, and includes a companion DVD to illustrate the techniques learned.

The S.M.A.R.T. Guide to Mixers, Signal Processors, Microphones, and More
1-59200-694-9 ■ $39.99

The S.M.A.R.T. Guide to Recording Great Audio Tracks in a Small Studio
1-59200-695-7 ■ $39.99

The S.M.A.R.T. Guide to Digital Recording, Software, and Plug-Ins
1-59200-696-5 ■ $39.99

The S.M.A.R.T. Guide to Producing Music with Samples, Loops, and MIDI
1-59200-697-3 ■ $39.99

The S.M.A.R.T. Guide to Mixing and Mastering Audio Recordings
1-59200-698-1 ■ $39.99

The S.M.A.R.T. Guide to Becoming a Successful Producer/Engineer
1-59200-699-X ■ $39.99

Bill Gibson, President of Northwest Music and Recording, has spent the past 25 years writing, recording, producing, and teaching music and has become well-known for his production, performance, and teaching skills. As an instructor at Green River College in Auburn, Washington, holding various degrees in composition, arranging, education, and recording, he developed a practical and accessible teaching style which provided the basis for what was to come—more than 20 books, a DVD, and a VHS video for MixBooks/ArtistPro, along with a dozen online courses for members of ArtistPro.com. Gibson's writings are acclaimed for their straightforward and understandable explanations of recording concepts and applications. Books in the *S.M.A.R.T. Guide* Series are no exception.

License Agreement/Notice of Limited Warranty

By opening the sealed disc container in this book, you agree to the following terms and conditions. If, upon reading the following license agreement and notice of limited warranty, you cannot agree to the terms and conditions set forth, return the unused book with unopened disc to the place where you purchased it for a refund.

License:

The enclosed software is copyrighted by the copyright holder(s) indicated on the software disc. You are licensed to copy the software onto a single computer for use by a single user and to a backup disc. You may not reproduce, make copies, or distribute copies or rent or lease the software in whole or in part, except with written permission of the copyright holder(s). You may transfer the enclosed disc only together with this license, and only if you destroy all other copies of the software and the transferee agrees to the terms of the license. You may not decompile, reverse assemble, or reverse engineer the software.

Notice of Limited Warranty:

The enclosed disc is warranted by Thomson Course Technology PTR to be free of physical defects in materials and workmanship for a period of sixty (60) days from end user's purchase of the book/disc combination. During the sixty-day term of the limited warranty, Thomson Course Technology PTR will provide a replacement disc upon the return of a defective disc.

Limited Liability:

THE SOLE REMEDY FOR BREACH OF THIS LIMITED WARRANTY SHALL CONSIST ENTIRELY OF REPLACEMENT OF THE DEFECTIVE DISC. IN NO EVENT SHALL THOMSON COURSE TECHNOLOGY PTR OR THE AUTHOR BE LIABLE FOR ANY OTHER DAMAGES, INCLUDING LOSS OR CORRUPTION OF DATA, CHANGES IN THE FUNCTIONAL CHARACTERISTICS OF THE HARDWARE OR OPERATING SYSTEM, DELETERIOUS INTERACTION WITH OTHER SOFTWARE, OR ANY OTHER SPECIAL, INCIDENTAL, OR CONSEQUENTIAL DAMAGES THAT MAY ARISE, EVEN IF THOMSON COURSE TECHNOLOGY PTR AND/OR THE AUTHOR HAS PREVIOUSLY BEEN NOTIFIED THAT THE POSSIBILITY OF SUCH DAMAGES EXISTS.

Disclaimer of Warranties:

THOMSON COURSE TECHNOLOGY PTR AND THE AUTHOR SPECIFICALLY DISCLAIM ANY AND ALL OTHER WARRANTIES, EITHER EXPRESS OR IMPLIED, INCLUDING WARRANTIES OF MERCHANTABILITY, SUITABILITY TO A PARTICULAR TASK OR PURPOSE, OR FREEDOM FROM ERRORS. SOME STATES DO NOT ALLOW FOR EXCLUSION OF IMPLIED WARRANTIES OR LIMITATION OF INCIDENTAL OR CONSEQUENTIAL DAMAGES, SO THESE LIMITATIONS MIGHT NOT APPLY TO YOU.

Other:

This Agreement is governed by the laws of the State of Massachusetts without regard to choice of law principles. The United Convention of Contracts for the International Sale of Goods is specifically disclaimed. This Agreement constitutes the entire agreement between you and Thomson Course Technology PTR regarding use of the software.